Table of contents

the Bike Path.

by Wayne Eliot Lankford

the BIKE PATH

the BIKE PATH

for Connie

Acknowledgements

There came a point in time when I realized I was writing *books*. I think I may have been in the fifth grade. Between then and now I've just been doing research, looking into subject matter. But always there was this inner voice telling me that being a writer was what I was going to be one day. It never relented. Since I was in college there had always been yellow legal pads around me that demanded to be written upon. People I knew, who sometimes I'd share my thoughts with, continually suggested that I "should write a book." Those yellow legal pads filled a suitcase and the lower dresser drawers, or they were stuffed away in cardboard boxes. Often they were left behind on moving days; frequently they were discarded. It was like kicking my heart to the street. I was too good at other things that I could make a living at and "everybody knows that most writers are poor." I had so many responsibilities to so many other people.

Then there came a point in time when I realized I was going to write *a* book. I found a page in Thomas Wolf's *Look Homeward, Angel*. It was my mother's book, she read a lot. She loved to read. All it was, this page I read, was a description of spring, the season. I memorized it. It lit a light inside me. It produced a feeling about life and so strong it was, it struck a cord inside me that still resonates even today. So, that was the moment when it didn't matter anymore what other people said or thought. It became about what my heart said. You see, I discovered that I had one and it did a lot more than pump the blood around. This heart of mine, I also discovered, was a pretty fragile thing—I broke it a few times, but it still works. It works just fine. Who do you thank for a working heart that allows you to feel so much of this beautiful universe? You thank the one who gave it to you, you thank God.

Then there came a point in time when I knew *what* I was going to write about. Connie Oden reintroduced me to bicycles and at about the same time reintroduced me to my soul. To my surprise, I had one of those too. I had always had one but somehow had lost track of it like it was one of those yellow legal pads. Connie showed me where it was and then one day she asked me, "Would you like to go to the bike path today?" The Bike Path. "Yeah, I'd like that very much." It was through Connie, her influence and love that I became introduced to people who inspired me, who made my life richer by instructing me about the limitlessness of the human heart and soul. Marianne Williamson, Deepak Chopra, Gary Zarkov and many others led me along and provided heaven-sent inspiration for what became for me a way simply to be who I really am, me.

Finally, there came a point in time when I knew *who* I was writing for. I had sent a few chapters to my older brother Neil who told me that some of the things that he read made him think about things he hadn't thought about since he was a boy. He said he laughed and he cried. My father, who really has only read parts of my work that have been in the newspaper, was most complimentary, saying that what I write about is so completely "wholesome" and how much that happily

surprises him. (It surprises me too Dad.) One day I'm unpacking my
bike at the trailhead and Barbara Malki sails by on her road bike.
She's about twenty yards by me and still pedaling, turns her head
back towards me and shouts, "Hey Wayne, I loved your book."
Barbara owns the bike store where I spend a lot of time. I had asked
her to read some of what I've written here because I wanted her opinion. When I first met her, the day I bought my first bike, she didn't
talk much about the bike itself. What I'll never forget was her
describing that feeling of exhilaration of going fast down hill and feeling the wonderful wind flowing all around you. I remember the one
word she used. It was "Weeeeeeeeeeeeeeeeee." What a deal-closer this
lady was. The thread here is that all these people have collectively
reached a point in their lives where they understand about life's priorities and have probably come to a place where they know personally
the frailty of life itself and how enormously precious it is. I think that
sums up the people who will most enjoy what I've put into words.
This is and is not a book about mountain biking in the end. Mountain
biking is the background for more than physical activity. All these
people who I thank here so heartily were responsible for helping me
not only to discover The Bike Path itself, but further beyond, the love
that is everywhere. Of course you don't have to be on a bike to discover that little truth, but it helps.

With that said I want to also thank the following people who,
whether they knew it or not at the time, were in some way instrumen-
tal in my going through with this process and without whose collective influences none of this might have been possible. People like my
kids, Julia & Paul Lankford, my riding partner Reed MacMahon,
Ron Moos, his daughter Heidi, all my friends and fellow club members of Birmingham Urban Mountain Peddlers, including Derrick
Seys and Bill Johnson. Further, in the way of acknowledgement I
have to mention mentors like my college philosophy teacher, David
Higgins and so many others including Mike Sorrell and Allen
McMillan, both of whom helped me to develop the communication
skills I'm finally now trying to better employ. I need to especially

thank and recognize Clarke Stallworth and Joe Kurmaskie who provided so much encouragement and invaluable mentoring. Really good friends like Dave Parrish who was always available when I needed his words of wisdom. Richard Hurt was there too, always in the background, urging me on to do what I'm doing now. There is a huge list of mountain biking industry people and their companies who I am most appreciative of for their commitment to this wonderful activity and who continue to strive to make it even better. Bruce Hyer, the Creative Director of Adventure LLC, publishers of *Hooked on the Outdoors* magazine, designed the cover and edited this opus. Without his expertise *The Bike Path* degree of difficulty rating may have skyrocketed out of control.

Preface

I believe human beings are naturally fascinated with things that have wheels—they've been around for thousands of years in one form or another. Two-wheeled transportation in the form we recognize as a bicycle is historically recent. Some credit Leonardo da Vinci, for a drawing he made in 1433, as the inventor of the modern bicycle, but most historians give the credit to Mikael Pedersen, a Dane, who patented his new Dursley Pedersen in 1893. I recently read that in 2001 the USA imported over sixteen million bikes and another 3 million were manufactured here.

I ride my mountain bike mostly on and around a mountain. I don't know how old this mountain is but surely it's in the millions of years. There are many other statistics that deal with the sport of mountain biking and there are tons of books about where to ride a bike once you have one. There are books and plenty of magazine articles that can teach you how to fix a bike when you break it after you've ridden it. There are all kinds of written reviews in print and on the Internet describing every kind of helmet, tire, rim, frame and any other individual part that together make up a mountain bike. There are people who can teach you to go fast, teach you to jump into the air and even fly for a few moments. There are places that will sell you a bike cheap and others that will sell you one for more money than you paid for your car. There are millions of photos on thousands of Web sites, hundreds of thousands of electronic pages about the wonderful sport of biking-road biking, cross-country touring and my favorite, mountain biking. There are races, trade shows, clubs and non-profit organizations all with vast resources of information on trail access, bike engineering, manufacturing and distribution and all matter related to the simple act of just riding a bicycle. There is no end to the number of books written about all these things and magazines that will keep you informed about all those just-described aspects of biking. There is nothing in *The Bike Path* about any of those things.

This book is about older things. This book is about connections. This book is about finding love. Of course it's about my favorite activity, mountain biking. While I was writing it I was able to draw from resources that are eternal, always available and inexhaustible. It's about a completely different world than where so many people find themselves right now. *The Bike Path* is a physical and metaphysical journey that travels backwards and forward into the human heart. These paths, these trail rides that I describe are more than descriptions of physical surroundings, they are spiritual places as well. Yes, they are full of the fun of mountain biking, but more than that, they are places to launch from into other worlds

Each chapter included here was selected by me for you to enjoy. Never hurry enjoyment, it's too precious. In fact, maybe the idea here is for you to learn a little bit about how to live and enjoy your own life more abundantly. In this book, I hope that, while reading the stories, you will find enjoyable these journeys along my bike paths. When these places cross your path, try pausing for a bit as if you

have been pedaling your bike along a mountainside path and have
come upon something interesting or beautiful. Take a couple of deep
breaths and ride along with me. Imagine yourself filled with peace
and let your physical body relax in such a way as to melt into the
story's surrounding, into nature and expand outward into the universe
while feeling always connected to your heart. Always strive to stay
connected to your heart. It will take you beyond my stories to stories
of your own. Savor your lifetime; travel it and see your memory
reconnecting to your own path images. You are a work of art yourself
made up of millions of brush strokes applied lovingly by a master.
Always remember that while you ride along with me. Life is about
experiences and this book is about some of mine. They are real experiences. Some of them changed my life because I was finally able to
pause long enough to receive a deeper understanding, an understanding that came about by simply slowing down.

the BIKE PATH

the BIKE PATH

Chapter 1
First Ride
🚲 🚲 🚲

About three years ago I was bored out of my mind from walking four miles four times a week around and around a quarter-mile walking track, getting nowhere. Then one freezing Sunday afternoon I got up from my comfortable couch and cable television and, in an almost dream-like state, threw my son's mountain bike, which he had not been on in over a year, into the back seat of my convertible and drove over to the state park near where I live.

I'd been out there before a few times with my kids when they were little and more recently with my girlfriend. We rode our street bikes on the paved roads there and at other places we'd discovered that fit our bike riding abilities. It was okay and fun, but not very challenging if you know what I mean. Over the years I had become somewhat fearful about trying any new activity at my advanced age, especially since I was a two-pack-a-day smoker and a beer drinker who was allowing himself to be over-served way too often. Something had to give. Either I was going to cash it all in with the basic heart attack or stroke in the next couple of years or I was going to clean my act up and do something about my loathsome, unhealthy ways.

Yes, I remember, it was a freezing cold afternoon, windy and as bright as sunshine gets. Putting the top down on my small convertible was the only way I would be able to transport the bike. It was really cold as I drove over to the park, with the top down, my son's bike riding casually in the back seat. I must have looked like an idiot to anybody who may have seen me that day. I remember looking back through my rear view mirror watching the front tire easily spinning in the breeze as I drove. I paid the two-dollar park use fee and parked my car by a lake near where there was an entrance sign to something called a mountain bike trail. It was twenty-one degrees outside, so the park was deserted except for me and a steadily blowing wind that had already numbed my face and my fingers. It had been cold for weeks and the lake was completely frozen over. Think about it, middle of February, twenty something degrees, top down, driving a convertible, mountain bike in the back seat, middle aged, divorced, overweight and smoking a cigarette. This is a picture of a guy who's lost it, on his way, literally, to the top of the nearest mountain, and is going to through himself off of it as fast as he can. The way it was, the way it had been, wasn't going to continue. I had drawn some imaginary line in the sand with an imaginary sword and told myself that there was no way forward save across this line. I was up from the couch, the cable TV and the monotony of the walking track. I stepped forward, grabbed the bike and headed for this thing called a Mountain Bike Trail. I never dreamed that this action would lead me to where I am now, but at least, I was on my way. I was on my way to something very different.

So, I get there, park it, get the bike out, get on it, and head for the trail and, just that quick, I'm on it, headed down it, headed around it, up it, over it and rolling, rolling, rolling, pedaling faster until I get to this hill and the hill starts to get to me and I can fell my legs aching, my lungs hurting. The sound of my breathing is so fast, it's filling my head and my ears, I'm sweating under my sweat suit, my heart is pounding and pounding, harder than I can ever remember but I keep going and going. I think to myself life is not worth living the way I'm living it, so what's the difference if I just die right here, right now—I'm going to get to the top of this hill on this bike or I'm going to die trying!

That was it, my first day of mountain biking. I had gone only about a mile and was totally exhausted. My legs felt like they were full of solidified concrete. I could go no further. At the top of a very small hill, less than a mile from where I had started, I collapsed in a heap. I threw the bike to the ground, almost unable to get enough oxygen to even stand. I bent fully over and went immediately to my knees, to the cold frozen ground, gasping for each chest-hurting, heart-pounding-like-no-tomorrow breath. I could see my heavy breaths move around the dust and the pine straw inches from my face. I felt the frozen sandy hilltop soil in my hands, I felt my knees pressing into the rocky ground. Then I realized it, as if a bolt of light-ning had struck me straight through my heart—I was going to live, and, though unbelievably to me, it seemed that I was going to survive the ride. God had heard me curse my neighborhood walking track and delivered me to the altar of mountain biking, where I suppose he'll keep me until I'm ready for whatever evolutionary step he has in mind for me next. What a day that first day was—I still think about it. The time I went biking and did not die

On my way back home that afternoon I thought about what had just happened, how really exhausted I was, how hard it was, and at the same time, how familiar the feeling was, and why. I had been there before, but instead of a mountain bike trail it was a football practice field. The feeling of exhaustion I had just experienced was the same feeling I experienced every day at football practice during the running of wind sprints and other conditioning exercises. At the time I felt that somebody was trying to kill me; it had been the same today, except I was alone. Yet there was this voice, my voice, inside my head telling me that this is what I needed to do if I wanted to stay here on Earth a bit longer. It told me that in order to live I'd need to work. Too, there was more there that day than the strain of hard physical work. There was much more. I was out in the open air; I was where they make the air, the woods. It was not all strain and work. It had felt so good to just coast down the trail, to pedal along in the flat places, to feel the elevation of the trail continually changing and along with it, the texture, the sounds of the wind moving around my ears inside the helmet. The force of my heart pumping blood throughout my body warmed my exposed skin. My face and hands were freezing at first in the wind, then they became accustomed to the temperature and warmed. The cold wind blew around the dry leaves everywhere and bent the leafless limbs adding to all this winter noise until where, at the top of a small hill, I got off the bike breathing as fast as I can ever remember, and I felt an new exhilaration, out beyond the pain of my straining lungs, over the force of my well worked heart. I felt really good and clean, a feeling akin to being reborn. I think maybe I was, because I was out there again today, having the best time, feeling so alive and connected to the earth and all its magic.

Remembering all that, I enjoy what it feels like now in contrast, just to be calm and connected to my inner self and my inner strength, breathing easily, feeling all the things that I had to learn again to feel. The things I'd so successfully blocked out, I was feeling as if for the first time. Some of those new feelings were painful to deal with but when you start to take the time to separate the important from the unimportant you realize you maybe have, at times, had your priorities misplaced. I have since become the interpreter of my own feelings, the feelings which I ignored for so long. I discovered that a daily quest to discover newness is something I am good at. I feel young today because I've taken the time to feel.

This book is about these paths I've discovered that I believe can lead sometimes to wonderful places. I feel I've been called to share my path with you. Your path, of course, is different from mine. But, think this through for me if you will, it'll make what follows seem, I hope, to better fit into your life. As you read my words here you will be hearing them spoken in your own voice. The words came from a place outside of me and into me and now to you. The images in this book were seen and captured by my eyes. When I tell you about them I'm showing you pictures in words of what I saw when I was where they were. They're not there anymore. If you get up right now and go and look in a mirror, what you will see is an image of what you looked like in the past. You and I live in the present but are able to go back in time as simply as thinking about yesterday. I believe we also have the ability—maybe just as easily—to go into the future.

When any of us start to recount our experiences to another person we are inviting them to share something we consider worth sharing. These kinds of things happen very frequently as human beings cross each other's paths. With that in mind try to imagine that there might be things with intelligence moving around you all the time. Things that maybe you haven't learned to see yet. Maybe those things have themselves moved into your sphere of discovery and are there now lined up for you without your conscious knowledge. Maybe you haven't fully discovered all that's there for you today because you are just too busy with a bunch of other seemingly important stuff. I don't know. I do know that right now you have discovered a stream of consciousness that once resided in my mind and therefore might be accessible to your mind. We are, you and I, at some sort of intersection right now. This one's called the Bike Path. You are invited to follow.

Who knows what you'll find just up the trail from here.

Chapter 2

The Bike Path
🚲 🚲 🚲

W e've always lived in turbulent times. The only difference in the fears of today and the fears of ten, twenty, thirty years ago, past centuries and yesterday is that the names of our fears keep changing. I believe a lot of people who believe they know better than we do, believe we need fear to survive. Without even thinking about it, and obviously we don't too often, we've just accepted this belief hook, line and sinker. If not, why wouldn't we have gotten rid of it centuries ago? It seems to me that mostly we fear each other. Every morning I walk to the curb in front of my house and retrieve my morning newspaper. Trust me, if you don't think you

have enough stuff to be scared to death about, you need only to start
subscribing to a newspaper. You have your choice of a bit of local
trouble or you can start the day being terrified of the global mess
we're always in. But the great thing about a newspaper is that when
you read it you're not at the same time bombarded with the audio and
video of the network news stations, who, in their pursuit of rating
dollars, I think will do or say just about anything to make you so
afraid of the world that you will even be afraid to turn off the set. You
can be led to believe even that the next emergency special edition
report may be broadcast live from your own neighborhood. What's
even worse these days is that the moderate, even-tempered newscaster
is becoming a thing of the past. All you get is one extreme or the
other with the video of the latest smoke rising from the rubble and a
quick lead-in to what some guy with an axe to grind himself has to
offer on this morning's events.

That kind of stuff is just not allowed out on the bike path. Stay
informed, read your local newspaper, never watch television news
again. Spend all the newfound time and energy out on the bike path.
You are the only one who can control what or who you let in your
head. Out on the bike path you are king of your inner thoughts.
Unless you get to a place where you can allow yourself the right
amount of quiet and relaxation, you may never become aware that
you had any actual sense of self that was clear and unclouded by the
needs of so many others, who, for their own selfishness, keep you
completely distracted from what is most important to you.

Out on the bike path you find your own way at your own speed.
You can race or you can coast, both are acceptable out on the bike
path. There are places out there, on the bike path, that you can stop.
You don't have to move at all. You can feel whatever you want to or
not. You can be, away from it all. Yes, there is this sense of being
away from it all that I appreciate. I love to hear the sound of my
wheels turning under me. Sometimes you can glide along and there is
no sound, your tires totally silent upon a smooth part of the bike path,
nothing but the sound of your own movement through the morning

air washing over you, filling your senses with a freshness that no money can buy, no human could create, something complete and infinitely pure and clean.

Moving along, your body and its muscles begin to operate themselves automatically, your mind separates you from the bike path itself and you can, if you like, drift right into another plane of existence. Sometimes this is what I come here for, not to even be here. Like being in a meditative state, you can allow your mind to expand outward into the universe, past vast star systems, defying all laws of physics and become then spiritually connected to an undefined source of energy coursing beyond all knowing. Purposefully you can allow your atoms to lose themselves among the stars, become transparent and spread out until you're invisible and able to merge with a higher form of existence, somewhere, just out there.

Out on the bike path my mind can be so wide open, so completely removed and free of the earth itself and all its problems, its confining logic, that my real being can rise and fall like a wave, like the undulations of the trail. I can become infinite and still be humbled by the beauty that is my surroundings until it is time to slip back into life, return to the rhythm of my heart, the wetness of my skin. Then picking up again the ever-moving vision, this reality that keeps me coming back for more, that satisfies completely a personal need, innate and satisfied here today once more, out on this well-worn path that other believers and I create just by following along.

Chapter 3

Going Tribal

T his morning I saw my shadow sitting on its bike. I had stopped for a short rest and a drink of water on a wooden bridge that crosses a usually peaceful creek. My shadow was cast below me on to the water. The water was still, as was the rest of everything else around so early in the morning. I was in a valley, what you might describe as a flood plain, with flat winding trails punctuated by many exposed tree roots breaking the surface of the sandy soil. The sun has a hard time making any headway here, as it's blocked in most places by a thick canopy of trees. This bridge, too, is mostly shaded except for periodic moments when the sun is able to penetrate the overhanging canopy of green.

These kinds of things change fast out on the bike path. I've been here days when the rain has come down so hard that I've considered turning back, afraid that the bridge might be swept up and carried away with me on it by a hard and sudden rush of quickly rising water. Then, other days, it's like this, it's as quiet as a church. Most days it's just plain peaceful, a beautiful resting stop for any traveler through these woods. I find it a very solemn place where I can pause, concentrate and more rapidly connect to the spiritual side of myself. Finding places like this to just be alone in, by myself, is a wonderful attribute of mountain biking that most people don't associate with this wonderful activity. Here, in these kinds of places, it's easy for me to go into a kind of meditative state, then, in turn, connect with the beauty around me.

As many times as I have stopped here in this same place, even at about the same time, this morning was the first time that I'd ever noticed my shadow on the water. There I was sitting on my mountain bike with my right foot resting upon part of the frame that formed the hand rails on either side of this twenty-foot span. I waved my arm as to say hello to myself. The arm of my shadow down on the surface of the water waved back to me at the same time.

Over time I've learned to appreciate the subtleness that the world offers up freely to those of us who will only just take the time to let it surface in our consciousness. Lately, I had been trying to live my life in what I had described to friends as "a more abundant fashion." This meant that many of my life's priorities had changed. Wanting to live my life more abundantly meant more than just discarding old bad habits of my modern way of life, it meant learning to look at the world through clearer eyes and without fear. My priorities had changed. After a while you can see that just about everything out there designed by man is designed with an element of fear attached. If you don't do something, something bad will happen. Truth is that bad things will happen anyway, the only thing you can do about that is change how you react. Good things happen too; learning to react in more positive ways about both had become important to me. You never can know what the next morning will bring, but you do have some power on how you behave and what you deem worthy of your attention.

This morning I was waving back and forth to my shadow on the water. Then it occurred to me that something else was going on. Resting there, my eyes drifted to my odometer, which told me I'd traveled just over five miles so far this morning. There my eyes caught and fixed on the two feathers I'd attached to it by sticking their points through a space where the odometer was attached to the bike. For a while now I had been decorating my mountain bike with bits of things that had caught my attention while out on the trail. On the front tube above the shock absorber I'd super glued the seven-sectioned rattle from a rattlesnake. I loved the noise it made as I sometimes bumped along the trail. Then there were the feathers starting to appear in other places on my beautiful ride. If the appearance of my bike reflected my personality, then it was obvious that the changing appearance of my bike might correspond somehow to the changes that were occurring in me.

I always kept my bike in what I believed was good working condition but had ceased any activity that included cleaning any place on it or part of it that was not necessary to its maximum performance. The dried mud on the frame and wheels hid the many gashes in the paint job created by crashes and the very tough treatment it had sustained as a by-product of my sometimes-hard riding style. I was one with my bicycle. I thought it was perfect. I kept it in good tires, I kept the chain dry-lubed to operating perfection, the cables oiled in just the right places and amount. All the parts were maintained as best as I knew how. In my eyes it could not look better. It seems to reflect the forest itself as it blends into the woodsy colors that so often frame it. Nothing needs to be added or taken away. Nor could I even ask for more in a mountain bike. This ride was, in its own way, a visible, tangible and unique statement about my commitment to this activity. My shadow looked good sitting on it too.

My ride looked nothing like it did in the bike store where it first spoke to me, but neither did I. We had both gone through some changes. Not so much changes really, more like we evolved. I don't know how it happened, but one day I noticed that I had about four or five black T-shirts. I had long-sleeved black turtleneck shirts as well, black shoes and socks and for winter I had long legged tights which I wore under black bike pants for warmth.

One day I was in another state and I went into a bike store and bought a black-and-silver-gray helmet and gloves. Expressions of nature were were finding their way on to my ride and into my life. My riding became more intense and more often, almost every day, rain or shine. My eyes continually worked the bike path. I felt the wind a lot. Then I felt it a lot more. I felt it when it was frozen and when it was so hot you couldn't stand it. To me it was all good, great, wonderful. Life had so many textures. I was paying more attention to those textures. Mountain biking had given me the chance to pay attention to the marvelous detail of the forest. At some point out on a trail ride just about everybody has to stop and rest for a while, recover and replenish. For me, those times afforded frequent opportunities to allow myself to taste and feel in abundance the sensations that are always there out on the trail available for all to enjoy.

There were many things to commune with out on the trail. Of course there were the animals that lived in these woods. They left their tracks everywhere. Storm and wind damage piled up and blocked the trails from time to time, the weather was the most obvious disrupter in the forest by far, sometimes felling huge trees with wind or eroding them out of the ground with heavy rains. Some mornings I'd come upon a rotting tree that would look like it had exploded during the previous night. This was good evidence, I learned, that a forest animal (probably an armadillo) had been searching there for grubs or other tasty treats. The fact that I seldom ever saw another human being didn't mean that there weren't a lot of them in the forest. They left their signs as well. There were these two older gentlemen, like me they'd park their cars in different places but always walked together and most usually got to the trail even earlier than I did. Two sets of footprints and walking staffs. I could see the same kind of evidence left by two firemen who tried to run the trails about three days a week. I knew their footprints well. These guys were both over six feet tall and weighed in excess of two hundred pounds, both of them had shoe sizes around twelve. Another cross-country runner ran out here ten miles before breakfast about three days a week. Start and finish the same place every day. He wore these extremely wide hiking boots with very deep imprinted soles. There were always tire tracks present, but after a while I'd learn to discern whether they were from the previous evening or day, or fresh, just-put-down tread marks in the dew-covered dust. I could guess how many and how fast and who they belonged to. I learned to distinguish between the serious mountain bikers and novice bikers by the differences in tire tread type. I could tell at a glance between the more expensive tires from the cheaper ones. One day I actually smelled cigarette smoke from two hundred yards down the trail. A day hiker was smoking on my mountain bike trail. What a sacrilege. I've seen evidence where it's obvious someone has for no reason at all destroyed the park's wooden foot bridges. In these cases the trail speaks volumes about what people do when they think no one is watching. Don't they realize that in the forest, someone is always watching?

There are many special places along the bike path like the one I was resting on this particular morning. The entire world is a special place, but in some places I sense I can feel a special connectivity to a higher being. Places where it seems easier for me to go deeper into my own spirituality and thereby connect more powerfully to myself, my own soul and beyond to an all-knowing source of creation and life. The action of calming myself after a hard physical ride by breathing deeply to lower my pulse and heart rate, combined with the conscious will to expand my whole mental being outward beyond my surroundings, then to focus back to an insignificant point like my shadow on the water, provides for me a vehicle to feel things beyond my normal senses. This action, out here in the wilderness, in this place over the water, is what I suppose some people might call, or might be a part of what they might describe as, going tribal. I clear myself of all tension and fear by thinking about cleansing myself of all tension and fear. I imagine these things draining from my body down through my feet into the deepest part of the earth. I see myself being washed of impurities until, after a time, I am as clear as fine crystal. Even my reflection in the water has disappeared. I become the morning light itself and can move with its speed throughout the universe. Or, I can become the morning breeze and move about the forest in all directions at once. I see the face of God in nature all around me. I know there is a part of me and in all living things, that can never die, that was never born, that has existed forever and will continue forever. When I pause like this sometimes I can think easily about such things.

Then, after a time, I open my eyes and see my shadow once again on the water. It's time to go on, I am rested and refreshed. This is a process practiced by my whole tribe. It is sacred. Be honored I've shared it with you. You can decide for yourself if there is relevance here for you. Know that as I go on from here, I know I'm not alone. The forest itself is with me. We were created for each other's pleasure. Both of us are constantly changing, providing for each other too the connectivity and nourishment be both need to survive. My appearance has evolved in this place and my appreciation and my respect for it increases almost daily. I believe that others of my tribe, trail riders and others are affected by these places. I hope so. I sense that my feelings are not unique. Many of us have allowed the forest to help us form our understandings about the most basic things deep inside us. Our appearances might even sometimes change in ways we might not even be aware of as our outlook and expectations are continually modified. Some things we can't see some days. Some days we can. The feathers tucked neatly around my bike and the moving dark shadow I become when riding the trails out here, pay respect, I believe, to the soul of this place that I am in communion with so often.

When we are connected together like that, sometimes we are like two beautiful voices singing the same song, sliding through the universe together upon wheels made of gold, light as a feather, feeling the power of even higher connections. They are the same connections that guided me to this bridge and invited me to take a look at myself for a minute or two, and then to look deeper beyond the water. Then after taking that special time, resurface, find again my reflection and see it wave one last time until I'm on my way, headed out into the rest of this wonderful day.

Chapter 4
Flick It
🚲 🚲 🚲

Flick It is a game I invented myself, but I bet that if you mountain bike very much you've probably played it yourself without even knowing it. I think you need to be in a particular frame of mind to play Flick It. You know, I love to mountain bike but some days I'm not as into it as I am on others. I'm sort of half there, maybe thinking about other things, thinking about nothing at all or just not sure about what I'm doing out on the trail that day. One thing for sure, it's usually on days when for certain I'm either not in a go fast mood or the trail conditions are such that a bunch of caution is needed, like mornings after a heavy rain, wind storm or both, the net result being that there are a lot of things lying in the trail that aren't usually, like tree limbs, sometimes even whole trees and rocks that have washed out in the trail or down from a hillside. A game of Flick It is perfect on days when the trail is naturally slow and intermittently blocked by storm debris. Of course, because of the size of some of the stuff that's on the track you've got no choice but to get off your bike to move some things just to get by. Larger things like large trees will be a nuisance for a few days until someone can come out with a chainsaw and make little ones out of the big ones. Flick It concerns the small ones.

The small things are always there when you look for them no matter what the trail conditions are. Every freshly fallen pine cone or stick is perfect for an impromptu game of Flick It, where the object of the game is to strike these things with your bike tires in such a fashion as to propel them off the trail, and in doing so clean up the trail at the same time.

You are probably already asking yourself why someone would bother to describe such a trivial activity. I, of course, have already asked myself that question. My answer is that there is importance in all matters. Hey, you might suggest that my time and talents might be better spent in the pursuit of other things. Obviously there are lots more important things to do than play Flick It. But are there really? I'm here to tell you that Flick It, in its extreme form, can require its participants to be in the deepest form of intense concentration just to survive the experience without injury. It is as dangerous as you make it. Just add speed to the process and you've got all the ingredients needed for severe injury or worse. Sorry, there is no pro-shop or green fees, not even a governing body to oversee, control or promote this great game. Just me.

I think it's only proper when coaching the fundamentals of Flick It to start with some advice on playing within a loose set of boundaries for the safety of the beginning player. In the beginning, take it slow. Don't go out there on your first day and try to flick everything you see as far as you can. I know it's a temptation, there's this feeling of exhilaration when your front tire compresses an object and the rear tire follows and as it passes over, say, a pine cone, and the rapid compression and resulting expansion of the object creates and converts motion to energy causing it to become airborne, which is the object of the activity. But be careful, campers! There is an immediate temptation to turn your head backwards and observe the energized projectile hurling itself through space. I grant that a perfectly flicked pine cone is a thing of beauty as it flies through the air end over end, but if you're watching it, and not where you are going, you could end up in a bad way in a hurry. Another rookie mistake is to select a target that is not in the center of the trail. The problem there is that, as you may be aware, the shoulders of the bike path are sometimes just loose dirt or sand. Get too far over to one side even on a straight path, get involved with the loose stuff, and just like that you're out of control. Out of control here means your flicking days could be over. Leave the edgy stuff for the pros. Use some common sense and the pursuit of becoming a skilled player and the sense of accomplishment that comes with it are yours to be enjoyed for years to come. Don't let your enthusiasm exceed your skill level. It will take some time to develop. Let it.

For me, Flick It is a way to just ease back into a place that does not have to be anything more than what I want to make it. Each solitary ride is a new creation in and unto itself, unique from all previous experience. The sound of play is a joyful noise. The sounds of Flick It are, to me, joyful. I don't need to look back anymore. Just the sound of a stick breaking under my tires and its parts becoming airborne, and those sounds as they fly and land back on earth are all I need to be inspired about this gift of life that enables me to even consider such things.

Chapter 5

Owl Town

🚲 🚲 🚲

Quite often the bike path leads me into a very wonderful place. I call it Owl Town. It's a valley where the trail runs along the top of one side of a mountain for about a half a mile, then downward to a natural draw and a hairpin turn. This leads you out for another mile or so downhill until you ride back up the crest of the mountain to the north and into another valley. As you move through this place you have to work pretty hard rising to the top of the hills but are rewarded with a couple of fast downhill rides. If you take the time to observe what's going on around you while your out there on the bike path it won't be long before you are meeting up with all kinds of creatures in this place. Deer are the biggest and therefore the most obvious animals out and about, but of course there are scores of squirrels, chipmunks, turkeys, birds of all types, seasonal snakes, one of the biggest redheaded woodpeckers in the world and owls are also fairly common. I'm not a professional naturalist or zoologist but I'd guess that owls, like most members of the bird family, have a certain hierarchy, or pecking order, that oversees and keeps things in pretty good order. Usually at the top of any group of animals, including owls, is a guy we call the Alpha Male. Specifically, here, in this place, I'm speaking about His Honor, the mayor of Owl Town.

His Honor, the mayor, is well-connected politically in these climbs, and has been for many years. Standing tall he measures about fourteen inches in height and about 8 inches wide. These are measurements I estimated as he looked right at me one morning. I remember my first encounter with him well. It was a very early fall morning, about six-thirty, and I'm powering my way up the left side of the valley when all of a sudden I see His Honor gliding along thru the air beside me, headed in the same direction I'm going, just about 20 feet from my right ear. His wings aren't even moving but he's gaining altitude and going about three times as fast as I am, coasting uphill and by raising up while in flight, comes to rest about fifty yards in front of me atop a rotten tree top.

The sound of his flight is very audible in the thick morning air. I'm amazed with this creature, with the effortlessness of his flight and way he just floats in total control to a landing atop a nearby tree. The tree he's standing on is an old pine that looks like it's about to fall over any second—already its bark has dropped away and it is completely limbless, leaning about fifteen degrees off center towards the high end of this valley. Quietly, I pedal my way up the trail until I'm dead even with His Honor who, to my surprise, has his back to me and just as I put my feet on the trail, turns his head completely around and towards me, now only about fifteen feet from my face.

A couple of days later I'm retelling this story to my father who suggests that what I thought was a moment of communion with one of God's creatures was only from my perspective and he suggested that the owl was actually just sizing me up as a potential meal. Most probably, what was happening was that the owl was following my movement, hoping my biking activity would scare up a chipmunk or a mouse for its morning meal. Thinking back on it I confess I was unable to detect any subliminal feelings of any cosmic connective-ness coming back to me from this being, but at the time, that didn't matter. I was face to face and only a few feet away from a truly majestic animal. Both of us stood there in the forest, me astride my mountain bike and him clinging easily to the top of a rotten pine tree. Mentally I thanked him for existing in this moment with me, making this moment for me, for us together, and with my voice I bid him a good morning and I smiled and complemented him on the beautiful town he lives in. I thanked him for letting me pass through and asked him to join me on my ride. Then, with his yellow eyes wide and fixed on me he turned back around and dropped from his tree, and spreading his wings, flew gracefully and effortlessly further up the valley until he was out of the range of my eyes.

To this day I still occasionally encounter Mr. Mayor. It's like magic sometimes. One time I'm going about 20 miles per hour down hill like a phantom myself. Then suddenly, my owl friend just comes out of nowhere and passes me like I'm standing still. Other times I'll ride up on him and we surprise each other, me slamming on the brakes as he jerks his wings to fly, takes off and lands again quickly just up the trail. I believe we are watching over each other in some way. Other times I'll see him high in a tree above me, seemingly overseeing all of his realm like some powerful protector of the forest while I enjoy the whim of his favor and am granted temporary access thru his private hunting grounds. I look forward to our meetings and I guess we've become accustomed to each other's presence. It's a pleasure for me to pay homage to such a noble sovereign. He is truly wise.

I admit it. By now I'm a bit envious of my owl friend and his abilities. He gets to fly and float through the air defying gravity and reaches heights most mortals can only dream of. He lives inside a miracle. Then I think to myself that I too live in such a miracle, for I can float and fly as well. Maybe not to the degree of my learned and wise friend, but certainly I go places sometimes unbounded as I float above the trail, wheels leaving the ground, sailing through the air in control and dominating in my own way the elements of space and time.

Our earth, the owls and mine, is a magnificent gift to us both and a part of that gift is that we have the choice to coexist with each other and with a multitude of other beings at the same time. As humans we choose badly sometimes, we forget that we are not the only creatures in the forest and forget that all beings have the right to exist in the forest no matter how different in appearance they are to us. We share together a boundless potential to be friends, and by sharing and accepting each others' differences, enhance and complement a greater and more enlightened existence. At least that's the thought my owl friend shared with me today.

Chapter 6
Blood Rock

W hen I was growing up we had miles of woods behind our house. They made for a wonderful playground, and they were always full of wonder and newness as we grew and explored deeper and deeper into their vastness. Early on we made up names for different areas and natural objects we'd discovered in our explorations. I remember Big Rock, a giant chunk of gray granite, that until I was about eight years old, I could not climb to the top of because my body was still too short to use the carved handholds etched in the giant stone by Indians, who, we believed, lived in these woods long ago. There was Hidden Valley, an area to itself in those woods which was characterized by tall pine trees that were covered in and surrounded by thick kudzu vines that went silver in the winter and emerald green in the summer months when we swung, Tarzan-like, holding on for dear life; sailing, swinging across deep ravines and onto outcroppings of grey granite which existed there in this forest solely for our exclusive enjoyment. There was The Swamp, that I tried to walk across when I was ten one frozen morning. I still remember the sound of the ice cracking beneath my feet and the helplessness of sinking into the ice-cold water, trying to reach the bank before the water was up to my waist. I nearly froze to death that morning. We swam at the creek and built dams and forts, we camped out, played Fox and Hounds and yes, sometimes we'd end up deep in the forest following our own well-worn footpaths on our bikes.

Just as those kids that I grew up with so long ago and had given names to places in our woods that meant or described danger or impressions of places there, I'm guessing the same kind of process occurred sometime in the past where I ride now. I don't know when the downhill we call Seven Rivers became known as that or when the Rock Garden became known as it is, but I'd venture a guess that nobody ever called the place we today know as Blood Rock until people started mountain biking there.

The most prominent feature about the area itself is the fact that a mountain stream flows right through the middle of it. During dry spells it appears like a natural spring because water is almost constantly flowing there. Looking further you can see a much easier path can be followed up the mountain if you turn left (going uphill) just before you have to get off your bike to traverse the rocks. Only an idiot would design a bike path through such hostile terrain. (Thank goodness for idiots.)

One morning this idiot was working hard again to improve his lap time. My regimen included breaking up the 17-mile loop into smaller segments, that over time, I could do faster and faster individually, find-ing quicker lines and hopefully better conditioning myself physically for a particular part of the course. Theoretically, I'd be able to put all these smaller segments into one big one and really knock a bunch of overall minutes out of my total loop time.

29

The place that had been most difficult for me was up the Blood Rock fire road and the place in general I'd always referred to as Blood Rock. My planning was paying off because I'd been able to stay in the seat of my bike farther and farther each ride up the mountain, shortening the time my ride took and therefore improving my knowledge and conditioning.

But one morning, as usual, and as foreseen, I dismounted my ride at the base of Blood Rock and began walking up the rocks, mindful of the possibility of snakes, slippery footing and just the overall difficulty of going uphill there. Feeling very fatigued and needing a water break I stopped and took a few well-deserved deep breaths and had a drink or two of the cold water from one of the two bottles I usually carry. As I rested there, catching my breath, I could feel the coolness of the morning air moving across my sweat-soaked T-shirt and felt the moisture roll down the back of my neck. For a moment there I leaned the heavy weight of my body against my bike and let my head drop to improve the flow of sweat from my face. And there it was, right next to my left knee, a sharp rock jutting out of the cliff I was climbing, just a dab of aged red paint the only indicator that this rock was any different than any other. It was not a place, I suddenly realized — it was a thing!

Looking at it there, examining it for the first time, I noticed just what a wicked looking blade it was. In fact, it resembled the blade of a crude rock knife jutting out of the mountain. With its edge so painted, it resembled easily a rock knife dripping with blood. As I stood there dumfounded to the fact that I'd never noticed it before, a chill raced across my body which shook me like a leaf, the realization that there existed here before me such danger that until now, this morning, I'd never even noticed.

I could see instantly that if you were traveling downhill here and made any kind of mistake, especially locking up your front brakes, your head would be just about in line to hit very hard a rock with a dangerous name. It was dangerous enough just walking here, one slip, one bad decision here about how to do this thing and you could be hurt seriously or worse. I wondered, how many had been?

I thought to myself right then that this place had been well named. I dwelled there on that point and let my senses taste this place for the first real time. There were spirits here, fallen bikers in pain along with hearts soaring in accomplishment. I reached my hand upon the rock and felt its strength and its warning. I felt myself change, again. I got more than a respite and a drink of water here this morning. My experience of this activity just got a little wider, fuller and at the same time more respectful for these surroundings. Blood Rock, with that little dab of red paint you could barely see on its underside, the way it was jutting out from the mountain itself, like a snake coiled ready to strike anybody who passed by here anytime, just added fresh new flavor to my inventory of textures and tastes. I'll file this one under Respect. Maybe cross reference it under Danger, but for sure it's going to be added to my list of Spiritual Places like Big Rock, Hidden Valley and The Swamp.

The whole experience of mountain biking was changing me in ways I'd not thought possible. I'd become not only stronger physically but better connected to myself, my spiritual self, the Earth, nature and the whole universe somehow, with new realization of who I was and who I'd been before, the same, but changed somehow for the better. I was constantly changing, as all of us are. I cared about this place known as Blood Rock, and more importantly, its bigger intrinsic value as an inspirational point for being, to me, for being itself.

Standing there next to Blood Rock I remembered that one day, back when I was eight years old, I had managed my way up a sheer rock face of granite and sat there at its top for the first time, able to view distances I'd never seen before. Today, this morning, I'd climbed another mountain, but instead of looking out, I looked in and was transported over time to my youth and felt again that glorious feeling of strength and the wonder of discovery, all at once.

Be careful out there on the trail always. Beware of the time machines. You never know where you'll find them. But hope you do. Be real careful of that one with a little dab of red paint on it. It can really affect your time.

Chapter 7

Mountain Biking as a Gateway to Metaphysics

🚲 🚲 🚲

For me, mountain biking is a gateway to metaphysics. It has three elements that just about all mountain bikers have more than a passing interest in. One: Mountain biking, (you're here reading this), two: Gateway, (that trailhead sign points to more than just a dirt path). If you already have a mountain bike and a will to ride it, in my opinion, you're already two-thirds of the way to a complete understanding of the universe and your relationship to it. Maybe you're already there. Yes, no, maybe, then one day you're riding down the trail and you see up ahead the trail forks right, left and goes straight. You go right, downhill. Well at least in the plane of existence you believe you're in you go right. Actually, you go all directions at once and a few other directions you haven't even thought of yet. You are riding around and all over and through a place called Quantum Mountain. Better check right now that your helmet is on tight. Go ahead and get that key out of your pocket in put it in the lock of the gateway (the gate that's not already locked), and lock it behind you. No, don't really do it, just imagine yourself doing it. Imagine yourself sound asleep, dreaming about sailing down the bike path faster and faster, the bumps in the road closer and closer together until the ride is smooth as silk, in fact the path is silk and you can see yourself from the other paths you didn't take, you can see yourself, the atoms that make up your self, your body, its physicality becoming blurred until you can see right through your speeding self. Suddenly, a thought goes through your head—going in a circle may be the fastest way to get to where you are going. Think of your last bike ride. Now stop thinking about it. Think about the ride I just described to you. Which one really happened?

Do you ever spend much time in your carport doing simple bike maintenance like fixing a flat tire? For that, you turn the bike upside down, take the tire off, put in a new tube, fill it with air, put it back on the bike, tighten the skewers and just spin the tire to make sure its centered on the fork. Isn't it fun to just spin the tire sometimes, making it go faster and faster, and see how long can you make it spin?

When I was a kid we would sometimes use clothespins to attach baseball cards to the bike and as the wheel would turn the cards would be struck by the spokes. We thought it sounded like a motor.

I rode my bike up a hill this morning that I'd never tried to ride up before. I thought it was too steep and too long. I didn't think about that when I started pedaling; all I was thinking was that I'd try to ride as long as I could without stopping and that I would just not try too hard. I'd take it easy and stay within my capabilities. All of a sudden I realized that I could make it and I did. I wondered to myself, why I had for so long felt incapable of doing what I had just done? What was I scared of? I wasn't having any thoughts about my accomplish-ment in any victorious way. My thoughts were centered on the rea-sons I had gone up the mountain the way I did. I was on a mission about something else, not even thinking so much of the feat I was about to accomplish. While I was climbing the hill my thoughts were someplace else and not on the degree of difficulty of the ride I'd cho-sen this particular morning.

I can still hear the sound of that cards being struck by my spokes so long ago. I mean, I remember that sound, the specific sound and I can picture myself speeding down the street where I grew up with a bunch of my friends, all of whom also have cards attached by clothes-pins to their bicycles. Together we were a thundering heard.

When you are out on the Bike Path you find yourself with many opportunities and choices. Theoretically it's possible for you to repeat the same ride you had the first day you ever rode a bike every time thereafter you ever rode. In the world of metaphysics all things are possible. I'm sure that I'd enjoy mountain biking even if the only way I could do it would be theoretically. But I'm pretty sure that I'm going to ride more often in the plane of existence I generally reside in, what I call consciousness. One day, some physicists suggest, human beings may be able to travel in time, theoretically. They reason that we may be able to penetrate these barriers in language not unlike the language of spirituality. We'll need to connect to resources that will enable us to do things we cannot even dream of now. It might be like moving into another dimension. It might be nice to become a stream of electrons moving faster than the speed of light. I don't know.

Today I did something I've never done before. It was a good day. After a few minutes of enjoyment I got back on my bike and rode down the mountain faster than I'd ever gone before. The experiences in this reality were pretty good. It was also good to think about a bunch of kids making homemade noise so long ago.

Chapter 8

In Defense of the Department Store Bicycle

🚲 🚲 🚲

I hear them referred to most often as Wal-Mart bikes but you can buy one at just about any mass merchandiser. Down here where I live you can buy them at Wal-Mart, K-Mart, Target and other sporting goods and hardware stores. They're everywhere. Wal-Mart has an aisle that's got an inventory larger than any bike store I've ever been in. My guess is that around Christmas the big retailers may sell more bicycles in one week than a first-class bike shop might sell in a year. Of course they are very inexpensive compared to what they keep in inventory at a real bike store. Out where I ride usually you don't see that many department store mountain bikes, but I know they're there. I find pieces of them all the time.

About a year ago a old friend of mine called to tell me that he had won a mountain bike. He explained that where he worked they had had a contest and he was able to exchange his prize points for a mountain bike. Usually I ride by myself but am always glad to introduce the bike path to anybody who is willing to try it. We set up a time and met the next afternoon at the trailhead. My friend, Derrick, told me that he has really been enjoying riding his new bike but the only place he's ridden it so far is around his neighborhood. I could tell he was enthusiastic about the whole thing but told him that I wanted to start him out slowly and safely. I wanted to make sure his first experience mountain biking would be something he'd enjoy and want to do again and again. Derrick was a good friend and would make a good biking companion.

For me, I could care less how much money somebody might spend on their ride. I believe that you should ride the way you want to, and being able to do that sometimes means that you might need more than, say, what I might require for the same enjoyment, maybe less. It's totally up to the individual as to what is adequate bike-wise to have a great experience. Starting out for the first time you'd want to get a big enough slice of biking to see if it might be a pastime you'd want to include in your life. That first experience, be it good or bad, will for most people determine quite quickly if mountain biking is right for them. It will also determine how much time and money they might want to invest in the future. I wanted Derrick's ride to be a great experience for him.

Derrick is in much better shape than I am, so I was surprised that he could not keep up with the very easy pace I was setting. Behind me I could hear him struggling with the shifting of gears and I waited up for him to give him a couple of pointers about shifting. Basically, I told him to just leave the bike in a low gear because, where we were going, the trail meandered around a lot and he didn't need to worry about it. I wanted him to just stay on the trail. That didn't work.

It seemed that whoever put Derrick's bike together had the brake levers in such a position that in order to brake, your fingers had to point almost to the sky in order to reach up to where they were. I can't really explain how they were. It was just a mess. I got out my hex tool and repositioned them. I remember Derrick saying that they were "a lot better now," and he didn't fall off the bike anymore after that, except for that one other time. Remember I told you that I'd suggested to him that he not do so much gear shifting? Well, I'm riding along and every so often I pull up and wait until my friend catches up to me, and pretty quickly he does. The trails where we're riding are very winding and it's easy to get out of eyesight of each other in a very short distance. I pull over and wait again but this time no Derrick. "Gee whiz, he was not even fifty yards behind me a minute ago." I turn around and just around the corner, there he is, standing next to his bike, with a very puzzled look on his face. The chain is off again. Yeah, I forgot to mention the chain—it came off four or five times earlier. This time, however, it's a new twist. Apparently, according to Derrick, he attempted to downshift while going up a little hill and in doing so, when the rear derailleur shifted the chain over to a different sprocket, all the force of his pedaling was transferred improperly to the derailleur, causing it to fold. Yes, fold and bend under the pressure of the pedaling of a 165-pound rider. It wasn't just bent out away from the frame with a loose chain. The bike frame itself was twisted; the forged metal bike frame was twisted like a piece of melting chocolate bar. The bike ride was over.

As we walked back to where our cars were parked Eric asked my advice about what he should do about his bike. He commented on how much he enjoyed the ride, except for the problems he'd encountered, and how beautiful the woods were this time of year. He said he could understand why I loved it so much. Then, regretfully I informed my friend that in order to get his bike fixed he'd have to get the frame re-welded and the rear derailleur was shot. Unfortunately the cost of either one of these remedies probably exceeded the worth of the bike. I hated to tell him that. This thing that he was now drag-

ging behind him, his reward for good work, it was beginning to sink
in with him, was now destined to find its way to the closest dumpster
on his way back home. He had picked it out of a catalog that only
winners got to see. It was the most beautiful orange mountain bike
he'd ever seen. He'd imagined himself doing amazing things on it.
Riding around his subdivision, speeding to the end of the cul-de-sac
and back. His imagination had soared! But that was yesterday.

I tried to stay in touch with my friend. I told him that he could
ride my other bike anytime and tried to get him out there for another
ride. It just never happened. He said he wanted to but had been just
too busy and put me off always promising we would real soon. It
never happened. Not long after that Derrick left the company where
he'd won the bright orange mountain bike. I gave him a call when I
heard about it and asked him what his future plans were. He said he
didn't know but just needed a break from it all. I told him I still wanted to go biking with him if he wanted to. He said he'd call me sometime. I'm still waiting to hear from him. I hope he's okay.

I remember another time that to me was even sadder than my
good friend Derrick's experience. One thing I love to see is a big
group of kids riding together, whether it be in the woods or on the
fire roads. I saw a group of about ten kids one day out on this rail
trail. They were having a ball. A rail trail, if you didn't know, is usually a very flat bike path built on an old railroad bed. They are a great
place to ride, very smooth and easy, easy on the riders and easy on the
bikes. By contrast, single-track mountain bike trails are very different,
they can test the strength of not only the rider but the very best bikes
made. Mountain bike trails are not paved roads.

One particular day I'm easing up and down the trails, gliding like
a bird and hammering it like there's no tomorrow until I see out in
front of me a whole group of people blocking the trail. I have no
choice but to slow down and stop completely. There are two adult
males and a group of about seven or eight boys of about the age of
nine or ten, all with bikes, all stopped. Nobody even notices me as I
come to a halt right there behind them in the middle of the single-

track. The two adults are deep in thought poring over what I take to be a broken-down mountain bike. It's in the upside-down position. Well, I'm standing there, a couple of the kids now noticing me and I hear one of the adult guys say, "darn Wal-Mart bike." All the kids are still and quiet. It's early morning and the trail is still wet from the previous evening's thunderstorm. I could sense this guy's frustration even with his back to me, shrugging his shoulders and exasperating breaths, "darn Wal-Mart bike!." Now all the kids and the adults finally notice me and the crowd parts like the Red Sea to let me by. I walk up and pass the group and out of the corner of my left eye I see this little boy. All the other kids are with their bikes except this one. He's standing there without a ride.

I'm sure his father and mother thought that the new bike they got him for Christmas last year would be a present he'd enjoy for many years. I can see his Dad in the middle of the night with his crescent wrench and screwdrivers studying the assembly directions, excited about what he knows will be his son's favorite gift this Christmas. The tire pump will fit neatly in a stocking. Maybe, he thinks to himself, his son's favorite gift of all time. Then one night at one of the Cub Scout meeting somebody gets the bright idea that they ought to take the whole scout troop mountain biking. Hey, every kid in Troop 393 has a bicycle. It'll be great! We'll go out to the state park. I hear they have campsites too! Who knew? Who ever does?

I can still see the watery eyes of that little boy whose bike it was that was cursed by the Cub Scoutmaster. I remember all their faces. I can see all their bikes. They were all from Wal-Mart. They were on the trail ride to Hell. None would be spared.

Think about it. Think about my friend Derrick's problems. In less than thirty minutes his chain came off at least four times. His brakes had to be adjusted and the brake levers themselves were put on incorrectly and were repositioned. Just a few inconveniences really, most of which could have been avoided with a little pre-ride maintenance. The problem with his bent frame was unusual and there was no real way for us to foresee such a calamity. Derrick lost his balance twice

and fell, just barely avoiding a serious injury. As for the Cub Scouts,
if you consider that their bikes were similar to my friend's, then all
you have to do is to add up the trail-ride-stopping problems of my
friend and multiply that number by the number of inexpensive
department store bikes, and you've got a disaster in perpetual motion,
or non-motion, as it were. People can't, won't or don't realize that
department store bikes are not designed, manufactured or really
intended for off-road riding. Or, they know it, but can't conceive,
imagine or accept that a dirt road or path could possibly be that much
different of a riding surface than their neighborhood streets.

They can't imagine it because they don't know anything about riding in the woods. Constantly riding over branches and limbs, through
creeks and heavy sand, dropping down suddenly where the trail
might be washed out completely. You find yourself left in a tapestry of
sharp tire-eating rocks and roots that chew department store bikes
like air. You know, the fun stuff! The very things that make this sport
so interesting for those of us who enjoy mountain biking like getting
through and over all the above mentioned hazards are the same things
that make you curse it if you don't have the right kind of ride.

Did I tell you about my dog? He's a sweetie. Yesterday evening
my doorbell rang and two little girls who live across the way came by
to see if my dog could come out to play. They're both five years old
and they come by every once in a while to ask if they can pet my dog,
maybe throw a few tennis balls for him to retrieve. I just can't refuse.
Even though they only live across the street and up a couple of hous-
es, they have the habit of coming by lately on their new bikes, complete with, for now, training wheels. Their bikes are perfectly matched
for their needs and are providing the girls with great enjoyment as
they wheel about the cul-de-sac in front of my house. My guess is that
these bikes will still be rideable long after the girls grow out of them,
probably in less than a couple of years. Then they might ask Santa
Claus for new ones. My point here, if you haven't already guessed it,
is that blaming a discount retailer for a broken-down mountain bike is
silly. What we ought to do instead of condemning their inventory of

bicycles, is thank them for their ability to provide us, the masses, with these very inexpensive bicycles that introduce the thrill of freedom and joy to so many, though not always on mountain trails.

My first bike came from Sears. My kid's first, second and third bikes came from Wal-Mart. If they'd come to me and asked for a bike store bike that cost over five hundred dollars when they were eight or nine I don't know what I would have said. Yeah I do, I'd say, let me think about that and let's go throw some tennis balls to the dog. Kids are so fickle. Their rooms are filled with junk that they never look at. If not for cheap discount store bikes they probably wouldn't even know how to ride a bicycle. Who of us would? Very few kids will actually desire a really good mountain bike. If you're a parent and you've heard yourself ask your son or daughter why they never ride that bike of theirs and they say they don't know, don't worry about it. That's natural. If you ask them and they tell you that they can't ride it because it's a piece of crap, don't get mad. Be glad because you are finished ever providing a two wheel ride to your ungrateful brat. But if he follows the "piece of crap" statement with "I'd like to get a real mountain bike next time," you may be in for an education and he'll be too old and too smart to help you go look for the dog's tennis ball. Actually the two types of bike stores complement each other well. The discounter sells only the introduction to riding bicycles while the bike store sells only the upper division models. They coexist quite well together for now. Let's let them do that and find something else to complain about. There are so many bike paths and only so much daylight. Let's not be snobs, either. There's room out there for all of us no matter what kind of bike we ride, and after all, the people who ride on the discount store bikes don't take up that much room out on the bike path anyway. Mostly they keep to the side.

Chapter 9

Rain
🚲 🚲 🚲

I don't know why some of us think that certain outdoor activities have to be put on hold because of rain. I realize that being struck by lightning is definitely not a good thing, but lightning is something that you shouldn't have to worry about during the majority of most rainstorms. It's usually just during the frontal portion of a storm system where any electrical activity is present at all. The potentially dangerous part of a storm front is usually over with in a short amount of time. It can rain for days without a peep of thunder. Nonetheless, many a mountain biker quickly decides that if it's raining at all it's not a good day for being in the woods riding a bike. I know. I used to feel that way.

Those of you who have experienced extreme weather out on the
bike path will have an opinion based on your experience(s) and may
or may not be in agreement with me about venturing out on such a
day. Most probably what trepidation some bikers might feel about
rainy day excursions into the woods might just be solely from their
own imagination without the benefit of actual experience. All of us
have cancelled outdoor activities because of only the threat of bad
weather. Most of us do way too much presuming about things we
know nothing about. What follows is one account of just one of my
rainy day riding adventures. On this ride the weather seemed to
change about every thirty minutes, so, it's pretty representative of the
different degrees of inclement weather you might experience. From
my account here you might better decide for yourself if trail riding in
the rain sounds like something you'd like to try. All I know is that
every ride I take is different from every other one. Weather is one of
the things that makes them different.

My sometime riding partner and good friend, Steve McMillon
and I had been wanting to go on a long ride for a couple of weeks. It
was winter, the first week of December and it had been raining off
and on for several days. Both of us had been too busy to try to ride
during the week so our only window of opportunity for the next few
days had narrowed to a Saturday morning. Over the past couple of
years Steve and I had ridden together a good bit and we both really
enjoyed mountain biking. As we discussed the ride over the phone
our conversation would turn to the obvious, the weather, which had
been so erratic here of late. We were hoping for a clear day, and as we
got closer to Saturday it was beginning to look like we were going to
get it. Yet, the radar kept showing these bands of showers coming
across the state like clockwork. It would get real cold, then it would
warm up and rain. By warming up I mean the temperature would get
up to about 40 degrees, then it would rain, and after the rain the temperature would drop to near freezing.

There comes a time with all of us that when we want something
bad enough, somehow, if at all possible, even if it doesn't make any

sense, we're going to get it. This is where Steve and I were, both of us suffering from cabin fever and a touch of light deprivation. We needed to be outside in the daylight in the worst kind of way. This daylight savings time thing was awful, by 5 p.m. it was completely dark this time of the year. We had decided we were going to start at the trailhead Saturday morning at 7 a.m. regardless as to what the weather looked like. It just wouldn't matter if when we got there it was pouring down rain, which for the past few days is how it had been about half the time. We were in that well-known winter pattern in the South so often described as, "if you don't like the weather, just wait a minute, it'll change." So we get wet, so what if it's cold? We'll prepare for it. It'll be great! We needed a mountain biking fix in the worst way.

Surprisingly, when Saturday finally arrives, the day starts off with a little sunshine early in the morning and as we head to the trailhead we are full of optimism about the current weather conditions, but also excited about the prospect of riding in possibly awful conditions as well. We just don't care. We're going mountain biking today. Turns out that when we arrive at the trailhead, it's cold, in the low thirties, but we've both got gloves and a couple of layers of clothing designed for the bleak forecast.

We start off with Steve in the lead, winding our way up hill. We take it easy until our bodies adjust to the cold and our muscles warm up enabling us to begin to feel our endorphins kick in as a direct result of this wonderful activity. Wow, it's wonderful!

The early morning light is trying to shine through the leafless trees of winter. The pine trees are full and green and their freshly fallen needles cover the trail in places. Their fragrance is everywhere. Suddenly, from off to the left, a huge mule deer darts up the side of the hill Steve and I are on and it splits the distance right between the two of us. The big doe just misses Steve and I nearly run right into it as it passes like a black flash up the mountain inches from my front wheel. Steve looks back and we both give a "what the hey" kind of yell, laugh and float on back to speed, leaning into the twisting turns, ducking the low branches, feeling the misty morning air.

Then with my mind well out ahead of my moving bike, I settle
into the calmness this experience creates for me and my mind begins
to wander. I start to think about my girlfriend. She was very concerned about our relationship. The night before she had told me that
although she cared deeply for me, she was concerned about what
course my life was headed, or to be more accurate, which way it was
not headed. I had just recently resigned from my job and further
decided that I couldn't even do the same kind of work anymore. I was
burned out, bad. Mountain biking had, along with some other major
lifestyle changes, created a new me that couldn't be a robot anymore,
I couldn't do work I was no longer suited for. Connie was very sup-
portive like she'd always been, in fact, she was in partly responsible,
as she had been in many ways the catalyst for my changes, my evolu-
tion the past few years. I owed her so much. She had pointed me to
places where I discovered a larger, fuller world, a world of grace and
spirituality, but one where my past livelihoods could not easily coexist. She had said that I should do what I need to do and agreed that
not being happy in one's choice of work was unhealthy. I was healthi-
er and happier these days but not without fear about all that was
changing for me. My past livelihood, although profitable, seemed no
longer to fit with my new priorities. I felt the changes in me that had
occurred would, over time, enhance all my personal relationships. I
still had faith in that belief, and knew too that good relationships, as
I'd come to define them, meant that there would occasionally be difficult periods of adjustment as we grow. All of us are constantly changing. Love, I've come to believe, when real, is a linkage between two
people that must be continually reinforced with caring and honesty.
Honesty, true honesty, can be so difficult to convey sometimes
because it requires accurate interpretation of one's inner self. My self
was elusive at times, during periods when major changes were occurring. In these times it was hard for me to focus. All I could do is pray
that each day a force more knowing was guiding me and I was putting all my trust in that higher authority. Connie was afraid of the
current uncertainty in my life and so was I. I was glad she had shared

her worries with me. I wished I had some sort of reply/answer/expla-
nation for her that wouldn't make her worry so much, but I didn't.
Her being worried was appropriate.

Moving up the trail a ways, Steve and I were making pretty good
speed, although how fast we were going was not a priority today.
Because of all the rain that week, the woods were pretty damp, but
the trail had drained well, it was in actually in very good condition,
hard packed and smooth. There were a few soupy places in the low
lying areas, but generally, conditions were fine. We were sailing
along, pedaling uphill and then coasting down into a small valley
when the morning light started to dim. And, as that happened we
could hear the sound of rain falling high in the trees above us. Like a
million small feet, the shower of raindrops rustled like a shaking bag
of beans. Even though it was winter, in these thick woods the high
limbs of the trees blocked all but a few direct raindrops that fell
meaninglessly as we pushed along the trail. Down below where we
were, just a little mist was all that was discernable, our bikes tires
growing small fishtails as we spun along the well-worn path. The cold
moist air felt good. We breathed it in.

Neither Steve nor I had, up until this point, ever gone mountain
biking in rain like this. Yes, we'd been through brief summer showers
where it's raining for a few minutes and then quits, or we'd experienced riding out of a shower into bright sunlight then back into rain,
but this would be the first day we'd ever have to spend hours in a
steady downfall, albeit somewhat blocked right now by the natural
canopy of the trees above.

As we rode along I began to notice a steady dripping of water
from the sun visor on my bike helmet. At our first rest stop, after
about four miles, both of us were soaked to the skin. We were cold,
but like athletes engaged in a spirited game of football, hardly noticed
any discomfort at all, our workout keeping us warm. Steam was rising
off both of us from our shoulders. What a perfect day!

After a couple of minutes to drink some water and catch our breath
we were back on our way, and as we pushed off again the rain began to

fall even harder. The sound of it falling increased as the trail twisted
ahead into a wide, flat sandy valley. We road on, crossing a few creek
bridges while the water rushed rapidly beneath us, almost covering the
crossing boards. The huge rush of water made a wonderful roar as we
passed with caution over its obvious danger. Our tires sank into the
sand at times; other times we would lift our feet as we coasted into and
through usually dry creek beds. The rain was really picking up now
and pedaling up a long hill the bike path itself had turned into a fast
running stream where we both laughed out loud. How humorous it
seemed to be riding a bicycle in the middle of a creek. It went through
my mind, up hill, up the creek, that's exactly where I felt I was. The
rain kept on coming, even harder now as we topped a tall hill and headed down the other way through deeper, faster running water, engulfed
by the sounds of this ever-growing storm.

There was a kind of storm inside my mind as well. I didn't know
at all where I was going. My life had been very good on the whole. I
had been very successful in my working career at times, but I never
felt satisfied somehow. I got so bored sometimes and though I tried to
make a friend of boredom and the monotonies of work, I could not.
So I looked for something more fulfilling. That is where I was when I
met Connie. I guess she saw something in me that to her hinted of
some redeeming qualities somewhere. I guess she thought that with
maybe a little work, they could be brought the surface. No, it would
take a lot of work and if I was really interested in having a relationship with her, I'd be the one doing it. I was the one who had been living so superficially, out of touch with my own spirituality and without
even the notion that there was so much I was missing out on, so much
I had the opportunity to gain. Boy did I learn, but that's another
story. Fact is, I did learn some things and pray I am continuing to do
so. I gained much, but know that there is more that I can do. It was
just that currently, my ability to produce an income to feed even
myself was, for the moment anyway, in doubt. My newly chosen path
was unexplored and therefore filled with uncertainty. Only time
would tell if the decisions I'd made were right or wrong. All I could

do is pray, to give the worry over to a higher power—that my out-come, whatever it may turn out to be, would be compatible with the Lord's plan for me as well. I felt like my chances were good, but I knew too that a lot of people were going to think I had flipped out.

With the rain continuing to fall as hard as it was, conversation between Steve and I had all but stopped except for warnings to each other as we became aware of things like falling tree branches, deep water crossings and, especially, increasing trouble braking. As the brake shoes picked up sand from the water and trail, a fine gooey layer of it began to adhere to the wheel rims making braking more difficult. The sludgy stuff acted like grease, causing us to squeeze the brakes harder and harder as we rode, but with less and less braking power. We had to rely on our front brakes more but that of course created more hazards to be concerned about as well. I'd seen too many people crash out here on good days by catching the front brakes too hard, locking up the wheel and go flying over the handle-bars. I once saw a guy do it on completely flat ground. It may have been me. On a day like today, it would be real easy to do. Another condition the weather created was it made the ground softer. Softer ground meant more resistance to forward motion. Fatigue began to set in much faster. But that was just part of it.

Despite all the hardship both of us were enjoying this crazy, wet winter wonderland. In fact, we were having a ball fishtailing and slid-ing through the turns. Braking sometimes meant skidding all over the place, like laying up your bike into a turn, sliding the rear wheel out left to go right and vice versa. Going through these swollen creeks as fast as we could spraying even more water skyward, hearing a contin-ual swooshing sound as we parted the down-pouring sea. What a trip! I was getting a kick out of just watching the stream of airborne mud flying up from Steve's rear tire as we tooled through the woods. It was flying everywhere; especially up his back, to such a degree that it was caking even on the back of his helmet. Yeah, and I could feel the same sensation on my own backside as I was slowly but surely being covered myself, head to toe in a coating of wet mud. Both of us were covered in the stuff and our mountain bikes looked as dark brown as the trail we snaked along. It was such a thrill to ride right through a two-foot deep creek that hadn't even been there the day before. The woods were saturated to overflowing and overflowing they were, water flowing down every hillside across every part of the bike path. There was no shelter from this great and wonderful storm. It was absolutely perfect.

I knew that outside of this existence things were not so perfect. Away from here, others I knew were troubled by other desperate problems of both life and death. They'd not all learned how to temporarily escape, separate themselves, become centered inside themselves, learned yet how to find the calm place, separate from the storm which ruled their every waking moment. They didn't know, hadn't learned that to be at peace took work. It took physical work like Steve and I were engaged in now as we both strained to press our way up this rocky hillside. It took mental discipline too, like the kind Connie had taught me through the practice of meditation. That was very hard for me to learn how to do; it took me years to separate myself from all the influences of the world, other people and problems we all have, all the time to one degree to another. Learning to separate from all that was hard, but somehow I did.

I was able to finally learn to and I made the time to go into myself routinely for peaceful, mindful rest, healing rest, and clean meditation. I made the time for what I was doing now, walking up this steep rocky mountainside, every step harder than the last through the rain.

The weather was taking its toll. It had set in on us almost unnoticeable then unquestionably Steve and I were nearly totaled out physically with four more miles to go. The rocks under our feet were slick and sharp now, all the once-surrounding soil having been washed away hours ago. These rocks gleamed treacherously, even in this underwater light, as we approached the top of the mountain and its swaying tree line. The fun part of this ride ended about thirty minutes earlier when we began a long, slow climb to the mountain above. Two hours earlier when we had begun this trek the sun was actually shinning. Yep, we had timed it perfectly for all those who wanted to be mountain biking in the worst possible weather, which I admit we did. I reckoned the rain had been falling the last two hours at the rate of about one inch an hour.

Just as we were approaching the top of this rain- and wind-swept mountain, I thought I heard other human voices. I realized then that we hadn't seen any other people all morning, not surprisingly given the conditions. Only crazies like Steve and I would be out in slop like this. About fifty yards ahead of us I could begin to make out a single column of about five mountain bikers beginning to head down the same rocky road we were headed up. As the distance between our two groups decreased I could see that this bunch of poncho-covered trail riders looked as worn out as we felt. It was odd, surreal even. Like us, their heads were down, just barely I could make out the tired and dark faces of other just-as-determined trail riders. Despite the uphill steepness here, Steve and I mounted our bikes at the same time as if to pay respect to these brave souls who'd, like us, dared to venture out on such a day. No words at all were exchanged between us. None were necessary. The sound of the all rain hitting against their ponchos as they moved past us served as audible witness to this ceremonial baptism in which we were all submerged. Under water, it was just like being under water. Then, I felt recharged as Steve and I finally made it up and over the last of the single-track creek to the fire road that comprised the last section of this day's ride.

We'd traveled about fifteen hard miles through this wet and cold morning. Up here on top of the mountain, about a thousand feet higher than where we started, I could really feel the cold and it was with some effort I was only partially able to fight off a case of the shivers. Just up ahead we'd be starting the two-mile down hill run. It would be dangerous today. All the sand had worn our brake pads to the nubs and going downhill today would be a challenge and a half. Unbeknownst to me, my rear brake pads were completely gone already, the steel pad holders themselves had been pressing against the sidewall of my rear tire and if I had been able to see through the grit buildup, I would of noticed the tire cords themselves beginning to shred. How's that song go? "Take it to the limit, one more time."

It is a good thing for one to know his limitations but at the same time not be bound by them. Actually, one of the things a little maturity will teach you is to pull up before you get all the way to your limit, but try to never underestimate it either. The ragged edge is nowhere to live your life. Later today, when I get down off of this mountain I'm still going to have a few problems to deal with. Difficult things often require a lot of work and careful decision making. Just before I pointed my front tire down the hill I thought about it, the fact that as I got to the bottom of this mountain, another one was waiting for me just below to climb. Hopefully I'd be able to connect to myself more fully after this ride. This had felt like a worthwhile goal in the beginning and it was certainly an achievement that both the Steveman and I would be proud of.

Doing the downhill was as treacherous as we had estimated. The path, a fire road, was a steep downward winding, red mud and rock, slick spot two miles long. Letting your bike get out of control for an instant could be fatal. Deep rocky canyons dropped off sharply just inches off the bike path to the right, and to the left was the sheer rocky cliff side that this trail had been carved from. There were seven creeks also to cross as we headed faster downhill, straining hard, pressing the brake levers as hard as we could to only barely control our speed, it being impossible to actually stop while going down this grade. Each creek ran like a river two feet deep and rising as we neared the bottom of the mountain. All we could do is head fast into the water and hope our momentum would bring us back up and out the other side. It was twice as intense today at about ten miles per hour as it was on a clear day at twenty miles an hour. Our arms were aching from gripping the brakes so hard. Then finally the last creek was forged and we were rewarded with about a half a mile of wide smooth red mud road. We sailed along, coasting to the end of the trail feeling like victorious conquerors. Then I realized that this feeling of exhilaration I was experiencing was why I'd come out here in the first place. I knew too, that Steve was experiencing the same feelings of grand accomplishment as we both rolled finally out of the forest together and into the parking lot. Seventeen miles in the pouring rain and we were just too exhausted to celebrate by much more than giving each other a high five and taking a long drink from the ice-cold water I'd saved in the car for this purpose. The outcome of this ride had been in question until we rolled there to a final stop. It would be a long time before we'd forget this ride.

Driving back home from the park, my mind reflected on what had happened in the last three hours and the space we'd traveled through. We'd worked hard and been rewarded with a certain kind of satisfaction that comes only from such challenges. I still had a lot of problems and tough decisions I'd need to make in the coming days, but I knew there was a higher power I could consult with for guidance. I knew I would do that. There were things that were fearful to me and I needed to confront them. Who knows, I thought, it might work out in ways I can't even imagine. It might just work? Just then Steve, who was sitting beside me in the car as we drove down the mountain to home, broke the restful silence. "Hey look! I think the sun's coming out." We both began to laugh.

Chapter 10

My Worst Ride Ever

🚲 🚲 🚲

A couple of days before I started out on my worst ride ever, I did a whole bunch of preparation to insure that I'd be able to meet some personal goals I'd set for myself. Basically, I wanted to improve my lap time around the seventeen-mile course I ride most often. To do that I knew I'd have to increase my average speed by a mile per hour or two and had thought I'd come up with a pretty good plan to accomplish that. It looked like the weather was going to be great on the day I'd chosen, which meant I'd have the fast track I wanted for my attempt. I had been working on my conditioning by doing shorter rides at a faster pace. I felt like condition-wise I'd found

a cadence I could maintain throughout my ride and with enough energy left over to really pour it on during the last two miles, a fast but
dangerous downhill. My bike was zeroed in and I was as comfortable
with it as I had ever been. It fit me like a glove. It was strong. It was
fast. There was just one more area I wanted to see if I could improve.

About a year ago I had bought some foot cages for my pedals. I
called them straps, they're like plastic cages for your feet. You use
them to better secure your feet to the pedals. They attach to your pedals with small screws and to use them you just slip your feet into them.
What they do is allow you to exert forward pressure on the bike pedals even when your pedal is moving in an upward direction. The theory (I guess) is that with these pedal kind of cages you maintain power
even when the pedal is moving upward thereby maximizing the pedaling motion in its entirety with both upward and downward motions.
Many bikers use clipless pedals, that I understand are a big improvement over the cage things I had, but they require you to buy shoes that
fit onto the specialized pedal. Evolutionarily, the clipless pedal is at the
top of the food chain in just about all types of biking. I just never got
the hang of the things. Moving up to the straps and cages was a big
enough step for me. If I were more competitive I'd go that way. This
time I was just interested in taking off a few minutes of my lap time as
part of an overall goal in my physical conditioning program. Mountain
biking was the major part of that overall process.

I recognized that when you change anything about the operating
mechanics of any process it requires a certain amount of testing.
These straps required a bit of practice. Just getting into them when I
mounted my bike took some doing. I had to flip the pedal over first
with my toe, since the weight of the straps caused them to ride upside
down naturally, then on the fly, slip the front part of my foot all the
way in until my toe was semi-snug in the apparatus. If you mistimed
it, or weren't quick enough, it would roll over backwards and you'd
have to try again. You have to do this by feel, because the bike is
moving, and you have to pay attention to where you're going or it's
pretty easy to crash. Then I'd practice with the other foot the same

way. I practiced this a bunch. I rode around my neighborhood streets and then moved my practice out to the mountain bike trails to where, with all this practice, I felt confident with this new ability and what I now considered an advantage over just plain platform pedals. I could tell the difference and knew I was better maximizing my efforts. I still wasn't one hundred percent with these things but I managed eight miles through the woods a couple of times practicing and was eager to push it through the whole loop. I felt I was ready.

The day came. As usual I was up early and after a cup of coffee, some orange juice and a bagel, I'd made it to the trailhead by six a.m. After pedaling around the parking lot and up the street for a couple of minutes, I set my odometer and took note of the time from my wristwatch. It was 6:05 and I was on my way. The air was cool and thick early in the morning and this was my favorite time of day. By myself I began my ride conscious of my goal and careful as I cruised my way around some tricky turns and lots of exposed tree roots that punctuate this section of the trail. The trap I'd sometimes fallen into in the first part of a long ride was to go too fast. At first I'd burn up energy faster than I needed to and be almost exhausted later down the course. Then it took me longer on climbs, or I'd just have to get off the bike completely, really killing a good run time. All these things and thoughts of things I did alone. Biking for me is mostly a solitary activity. The rest of the world could care less about what I was doing or why really I did these kinds of things in the first place. I've never cared if they cared, this was for me, not for the outside world. I was by myself out here. It was my bike, the trail and I. I loved it so much. It was a form of moving meditation, all this space, this air, all these trees, plants, grasses, creeks, bridges, animals, all belonged to me and were part of a universe filled with wonder.

After a while I realized that I was moving pretty good. My bike was tuned to perfection. My gear changes were often and smooth, the way they need to be to maintain higher speeds. My brakes were just right as well; I would almost lock up my rear tire and downshift at the same time coordinating purposefully to finesse my way over difficult terrain, sharp turns and difficult surfaces. Speed was my friend today. As I moved along so quickly my perspiration mixed with the wind of my flight produced an air conditioning effect that kept me cool despite the warming sun. I was in control, fast and focused on the trail. At six miles into the ride I looked at my watch and to my surprise discovered I'd traveled those first six miles in just about 30 minutes. With a pace like that, if I could maintain it, I'd be well inside of the time I was shooting for. I had tons of energy and like they say, my heart was soaring.

Continuing along the trail I was beginning to feel my energy starting to wane somewhat so I knew it was time to start putting some fluids into my body. Still moving along I reached down and selected one of the two bottles I carried. I went for the water bottle. The other is full of a sports drink. I noticed right away that the bottle, which was completely frozen an hour ago, was now completely thawed, a sign to me that maybe it was a little hotter out this morning than I predicted. Then it happened. As I reached down to put the bottle back in its cage I managed to let my front tire veer off just a bit to the left as I was turning at the same time. It was a gentle turn but I was just enough off center to find my way into the soft sandy shoulder and my front tire just sank right into it. This twisted my wheel hard left while my momentum was still carrying me forward. The result was a classic example of Newton's third law — my body, which was in forward motion, was going to remain in motion even though my bike was to take a hard left. If I'd been able to, all I needed to do was just put my foot to the ground and retain my balance just enough, but my feet were frozen into the straps. I was going over the handlebars down the hill and there was nothing I could do about it. There I was, just for a moment, maybe a whole second; I was able to stop the bike completely. I balanced there completely still, my feet trapped in the straps and my body weight about to tumble forward. It's a moment I'll not forget because in that moment I realized that before I was going to hit the ground my right upper body was going to plow hard into the side of an oak tree that was down the hill about five feet off the trail. I let go

of the handlebars and attempted to break my awkward fall but was
only partially successful

My rib cage took most of the impact as I ended up face down at
the trunk of the tree, in the dirt headed down a hill. Face down,
breathing hard but shallowly because of this new pain all over my
upper body. I remembered at last that the first thing you do in a situation like this is to not move, or try not to move. I took inventory and
ultimately decided to slide my legs off my bike and using the hillside,
try to roll my body over, letting gravity do the work. In a minute I
was sitting there trying to inventory my wounds. I decided after a
while that my ribs were probably not broken and only bruised slight-
ly. I was skinned up pretty good with a little blood from both knees
and my left elbow got scraped up too somehow. Mostly I was worried
that this delay was going to wreck what was a great ride till now. I
managed to get to my feet and back to the trail where I put my upper
body through a couple of turns and stretches. I decided that I'd be
sore but could continue. My bike was fine.

The thought occurred to me that trying to go fast from here on
was probably a bad idea. In fact, as I took a painful deep breath after
a long drink of water, I considered quitting altogether for the day. But
then, even hurt, I might still be able to record a good time for myself.
I decided to go on. I hurt a little, but so what.

After a couple of more miles I was glad I hadn't given up. It was
still early in the day and what else did I have to do? This was my
favorite place on earth and out here all was good. How long it took
me to ride this thing became less and less important the further along
I traveled. The bike path is where I live. Its my home, its my temple
and in my temple instead of getting on your knees you move them and
by doing so you become part of the place. My confidence was acceler-
ating as fast as I was. Most of the earlier pain was behind me. I
looked at my watch and my mileage and realized I hadn't lost that
much. I was making it up fast and as I rose slowly but surly up a hillside felt that I was in complete control of this day.

Maybe that's what I love about mountain biking so much. The

trail is different every day. Today it was changing even as I rode upon it. Just as I was about to approach a new zenith in self-confidence the ground seemed to move once more the wrong way and again I locked up in those stirrups, I plunged down another hillside like a runaway surfboard over an ocean of rocks. I heard the sound of the rocks crunching underneath me as I slid further and further down the mix of pine straw and gravel, finally coming to a halt just in time to see my bike stop neatly next to me.

The main reason I go mountain biking so early in the morning is I like to be out there by myself. It's easy to get the feeling that this whole place is my personal property and all others are only allowed to ride there by my expressed permission. It's my sanctuary of peace. Out here in the forest I've discovered places where I believe the connectivity to the universe is stronger. In those places I feel I'm able to let negativity drain from my being and in turn tap into powerful resources that strengthen my soul and my spirit. It's a real thing to me. For me, there is no better place to mentally cleanse myself. I get out there, find one of my quiet places and let nature have me. I surrender my self to God and melt into and beyond all matter and space. Where I crashed was not one of these places.

Thankfully, I'm not hurt too badly, just a few more scrapes and scratches. I'm wearing a black shirt and black shorts that, as I inventory again, are both torn a bit, but are mostly covered with the dust that was churned up as I slid through the gravel. I'm OK but my ribs are smarting much worse. If I wasn't already well past the halfway point, the point of no return, I'd definitely turn it around down the hill and just try to find a ride back to my car. I have no choice now. I have to go on. The problem is that the next part of the trail is the hardest part of the trip. I'll really have to take it easy if I'm going get over the next mountain. Every step hurts my ribs and for some reason right now the slightest hill takes more effort than I ever expected. I'm thinking I still have five miles to go, but just the next two are uphill when I remember there is a fire road just ahead. If I take the fire road it should be a lot easier than the uphill single-track. That's what I decide to do. I'm going to get through this thing just fine. Alas, I can forget about that personal best time for this day. My watch tells me I've already been out here for an hour and a half.

About a half an hour later I come off of the single track to where it crosses the park road that leads up to the top of the mountain and to where it then joins up with a fire road that is part of the mountain bike trail. I'm pretty unfamiliar with this road but I've been up it before and distinctly remember where it joins up with the bike path. I have a clear picture of that in my mind. Not far up the road it begins to wind out to the west the exact opposite direction to where I need to go. I think to myself that this is the way all mountain roads are, they always meander some. But besides that it appears to be a whole lot steeper than I remember. The only other time I'd been up here was in a car. It's getting hotter by the minute. I've left the sanctuary of the forest and the shade of the trees and am now more in sunshine than not. I'm hot and I have to drink and rest more often. I'm finding myself leaning over my bike, bent at the waist, I see my sweat dripping down to the dusty road, it's pouring off of me. Real soreness is starting to seep into my ribcage. It's very hot. There's nobody around. There's no flat ground. I have to keep going. I've got to get to the top, get to the fire road, the flat ground and the coolness of the shade. I need cool air moving over my soaking wet body.

Taking the park road was the worst idea I'd ever had. Ultimately it took me two miles out of my way and in doing so just about drained every ounce of energy I had left. Instead of less than two hours this ride was destined to take an extra hour, but I made it to the fire road and was rewarded with an easy glide down a gentle slope, which was the top of this mountain I'd just climbed the hard way. My ribs were beginning to ache a bit more and I could feel acutely every bump in the road. But I knew the end was only four more miles down the road and the last two miles were completely downhill. I was trudging at this point, wondering how I ever would have thought that those pedal cages could ever be an improvement for me. They had been my undoing and for now I had them upside down, banished to the underside of my feet. For safety's sake I would have to turn them upright later on so as not to catch them on a root or rock and really make a worse day than what I was already having. I vowed "never again" and the first thing I was going to do after a nice long rest was to take these stupid things off my bike and trash them.

I'm nearly exhausted and really taking my time at this point. I've just got a sip or two of the sports drink left and trying to make it last until I get to the place where the last downhill starts. It's really hot out here and so am I. The top of the mountain road is mostly in the sunshine and I know that there won't be any real relief from this heat till I get home. But I'm starting to be encouraged. Just up ahead I see where this road begins to slide downhill again and I can take a rest from the cranks and coast a while. I'm doing this and all of a sudden I feel this sharp pain on my right arm just below my elbow.

Ouch! I lift my arm up and out and there is this huge horsefly stuck on my arm and there's blood dripping down my elbow, my blood. Apparently I've been bleeding there since my last wreck and hadn't noticed it what with all the other bangs and bashes I'd suffered. I swatted the fly away and kind of laughed to myself through the pain and thought what else can happen? It was funny now. I thought of what I must look like. Filthy of course, drenched in sweat, at the limit of my endurance and bleeding, a ready target for horseflies. If I stop one more time I'm sure I'll look up and find buzzards circling overhead. Got to keep moving, almost home

The two-mile downhill was, thankfully, pretty uneventful. I took it real easy, and where earlier in the day had imagined myself speeding down those hills like a maniac, I was content now to just to ease down this most dangerous part of the whole trail. Even here I was picking out new sources of pain. Having to compensate for my injured ribcage, I'd put more weight on my arms than normal and they felt like lead. I wished to myself I could just drop them to my side but I had to stay on the brakes to slow my decent.

I thought to myself how good it would feel to just fall forward into a heap somewhere. As my thoughts began to center on being finished with this ride I began to feel a since of pride with myself. I could have turned back after my first crash and just called it a day but I had chosen to push it forward. This activity, despite all the problems I was having today, had become part of me. I was a mountain biker. Sometimes I think before anything I am a mountain biker. I realize to most that doesn't seem like a heck of a lot, but to me it's a point of some pride.

I finished out the last half a mile with my hands by my sides, only raising my arms and hands to the handlebars for turning and brakes; that way I coasted up onto the pavement across the street where I'd parked my car three hours earlier.

There were a few people just getting ready to start their own journey up the mountain. I coasted up to the rear of my car and in a fluid motion stopped the bike, got off and lifted my bike on to its carrying rack. A mountain biker was behind me and just about to head out when he slowed down next to me and asked me how the ride was this morning? I didn't even think about it before I answered, "It was fantastic! It was the best ride I'd ever had."

Chapter 11

Don't Try Me To Try
The Moon

🚲 🚲 🚲

For much of my life friends have told me that I should write a book. They always seem so enthusiastic when they say that but when I ask them what I should write this book about, what subject matter I should explore, they don't seem to be able to provide any viable suggestions. And of course that's the hard part. Nonetheless you should know that I have had a few ideas about that. This morning while out on the bike path, for no good reason, this whole subject started passing through my mind. That's what I love about mountain biking. For somebody like me it's so conducive to my thought processes.

Yeah, this morning it was absolutely beautiful. Everybody I passed on the trail today was in such a good mood it seemed. Everybody I met on the path exchanged a good-morning greeting and commented on "what a beautiful day" it was. I had to agree. If it's actually true that some days are more perfect than other days then this morning was an example of the more perfect variety. I was light hearted and the hills were easy.

Then, out of nowhere, I began to laugh out loud thinking about "The Pigeon Wars," an idea I had for a book a long time ago. One of my creative ideas?

The main character of The Pigeon Wars was a pigeon named Joe. When I introduce my readers to Joe the war has been ended for many years. Joe is very old, a partly disabled, (walks with a pro-nounced limp presumably because of war injury) alcoholic, blind in one eye, lives as a scavenger of the parking lot of a downtown Atlanta junk food Drive-In called the Junk Food Drive-In.

Joe had the bad habit of going up to complete strangers and threateningly demand they listen to him. Sometimes, he'd cry on his knees while begging strangers to believe him and his warnings about the imminent danger their brains were in. Joe was convinced that aliens from outer space had invaded earth. He believes they've come here because they have developed a taste for human brains. They eat them. They want to eat our brains. They like the way our brains taste. On their planet, we, our brains, are a delicacy. These aliens don't feel a single iota of guilt about it either, because to them, the way they see it, is why not, we weren't using these organs anyway. Who would really care? Well, Joe eventually teams up with another pigeon named Fred and they don't save the world, but they are able to corner the market in off-world brains, at least for a while.

In the later chapters the aliens' equivalent to the Food and Drug Administration discovers that there is a genetic marker in human brains that indicates that we, earthlings, are, as too are the inhabitants of the planet Zog-row, direct decedents of tuna fish. So, by the long-existing law not to consume relatives, all consumption of human brains is forbidden and new golf tournaments are conceived to improve relationships between Earth and Zog-row.

I probably shouldn't have told you how the story comes out but it's the only way to be sure you won't bug me about it sometime in the future. I mean those of you who will still have title to your own brain. See, making it illegal just made people want to do it more. See what happens when people don't mountain bike. You think that Joe was a sad case? You should get a look at the millions of helplessly addicted Zogrovians. Brains, brains, brains, that's all they can think about. It's so sad.

Another idea that nobody else would suggest to me was to rewrite a classical novel updating it to the present day and giving it a meta-physical twist. I had spent a full year and wrote sixty thousand words when I decided maybe that wasn't the best idea I ever had. If you ever decide to blow your brains out, forget the gun. I got the real deal over here in a desk drawer, hand written on nine yellow legal pads, sixty thousand words. It's called, *Moby Dick, From the Whale's Perspective*. I need to further warn you that this opus contains a bunch of dream sequences and at some point even I couldn't keep it straight, what was actually happening and what was really a dream. I figured because it was all pure fiction that it didn't really matter anyway. But then I never reckoned that I would start to receive subliminal mes-sages from between the yellow spaces where the words were written and the blue lines that were pre-printed on the pencil pads. For some reason I can't seem to throw the thing away nor can I even open that drawer where it sleeps. Yeah, I'm sure it's asleep.

There were years spent in smoky barrooms having philosophical discussions that turned into divine inspiration and I churned out the lyrics by the wheelbarrow full to country and western songs. Maybe you remember, "You Can't Get a Dead Man Drunk," "This Land Is Not Your Land So Get The Hell Out," "They Can't All Be Million Sellers" and everybody's favorite, "Incest Love." I was drowning in a sea of negativity. I thought myself a serious writer and the world was full of contemporaries who were just as serious as I and untalented as I was but who were making a living at it. In those days, by day, all day long, inside my cubicle at my straight job, my ideas flowed like burning lava, or maybe it was plastic vomit, while at the same time I analyzed corporate financial statements to supplement my earning as an artist. I scanned the annual reports looking for poorly explained anomalies, solvency, efficiency and profitability ratios out of the norm. I pounced on a financial weakness like a lion on a gazelle. "Assets are disproportionately centered in inventories and accounts receivables. Inventory turn is sluggish and day's sales outstanding are three times the norm for this industry. Debt is heavy in relation to worth. The above slowness reported by creditors is noted, and an unbalanced condition prevails. Further analysis is deferred until more recent and representative figures can be obtained." Yes, I was chained during the day to an oar which I pulled in unison with the rest of the Brooks Brothers-suited twenty-five year olds dreaming of freedom above the shifting decks and beyond. That was a time in my life when the thought of mountain biking had never even occurred to me. Life was passing me by.

So much was expected of me. At one point I gave up song writing and started doing portraits, mostly in charcoal pencil. I set up shop in the park next the tarot card readers. As low a rent district as you can get in the art world. On the other side of me two black kids tap-danced and played the tambourine. Oh, how I wished I could dance. Those two made a fortune. Still, by day, I could not break the shackles of corporate cowboyism to which I was bound so tightly. To this day I still haven't used up all those sky miles. All these creative things I tried. In all I tried I was creative. I've devoted a lifetime to doing things, whatever they were, just a little bit differently. And I fell short every time because when I tried I tried for the moon; I did not realize that the moon was never my intended mission. My path was always somewhere else. It was always right beneath my feet, in the dust, in the dirt, in the mud, the leaf and pine straw covered bike path that twisted and curved so near but invisible to me. Invisible to me because I mistakenly believed that my creativity was enough in itself to propel me to the places I wanted to go. I forgot who endowed me in the first place with such wonderful gifts. I ignored my own spiritual self and its connection to much higher sources of power.

That corporate world I used to be such a part of and was such a part of me is no longer part of my everyday existence. All during those years I dreamed of escape. I was very good at what I did and I enjoyed a lot of success but, like I said, it never quite satisfied me. It didn't satisfy me because the part of me that needed to be satisfied could not be reached by things out there in the world. I believed that everything that existed did so and was self-evident by its tangible existence alone. I thought very little about an invisible other world of spirit. I lived in an Isaac Newton world of physics and actions, a Copernican universe of absolutes. Very cold place, the Copernican universe, often so clouded by cigarette smoke and alcohol fumes, the lingua franca of the business world.

How many lives did I have to live to learn the lesson of a lifetime? How many had I lived already? Those are common questions asked in some cultures of the world. Here in the USA we seem to be pretty unquestioning about our religion. Most of us, especially here in the Southeast, just don't get a chance to be exposed to anything other than the religion of our parents. Unintentionally I'm sure, but nonetheless true, we're not taught anything about other cultures' belief systems, therefore because we don't know anything about them, we tend fear them. We believe if you don't believe like we believe you are going to the devil.

Yeah, all this stuff I think about out on the bike path. I know I'm not the only one. I don't mean to say or suggest that out in the forest mountain biking is a better place than anywhere else to meditate or think about such things. I'm just reporting that to me, I've found it quite accommodating. Out there I think I can better observe not only what surrounds me but what I too surround. I mean I can expand myself anywhere now at just about anytime, but out on the bike path it's easier for me. My spiritual self had been developing all my life, always there under the surface of my life's activities. That's something that I today readily accept as an absolute truth for myself. In the same way I've learned that absolutes are a dangerous thing. Accepting other people's absolutes can get you into a bunch of trouble. You need to be real careful about what you believe in these days. It's always been that way, but today, you are the one making the decisions about your own life's path. I just think that all of us need to be a bit more deliberate about what decisions we make that affect our path. I say that because I made some wrong ones and they cost me a bunch of years of heading in the wrong direction.

There are just too many influences out there, off the bike path, that attempt to sway our thinking. When I'm confronted by such influences or a person, whether they be a teacher, preacher, politician, newscaster or whatever, I just try to determine if they are trying to scare me into thinking like they think or do they seem to be caring and at peace with themselves. Do they make me mad or do they make me care? Are they about fear or are they about love? If they say they are about love but all they talk about is fear, what are they really about? If they suggest they are about the right way to live but only talk about the wrong way, what are they about? Tough questions and hard to easily answer. I just seems to me that we human beings spend a disproportionate amount of our precious time being taught to fear stuff instead of how to understand and not be so fearful.

Look at us, we line up for it every day for it in front of our television sets, the radios in our automobiles and in my case, the morning newspaper. "Okay, let's see here, what do I need to be afraid of today?" Yeah, lots of good things, there's the war on terror, some kind of virus, the stock market. Boy, life sure was a lot easier when we could blame everything on the Russians. I sure miss those days.

The thing is that, what I believe is that, all these things we are suppose to be fearful about are just the things we are afraid of now. The things we've selected as sort of a soup de jour, fear de jour. Unless we really change what's important to us we are in for more fearful living until of course, we scare ourselves to death literally. We can become so afraid of others that, they sensing our fear of them, begin to fear us equally and believe we are out to get them like they

are out to get us. We get to the point that we both need to get other
first or we won't have a chance. All because our way of thinking is so
right and their way of thinking is so wrong. What a mess!

No messes or such foolish thinking is allowed out on the bike
path. Well maybe a little silly thinking would be OK. Do this for me.
Think of it as a mental exercise. That's what it is. Picture a person in
the world who you are afraid of for whatever reason. If you'd rather,
pick a bunch of people who you fear. It won't matter. Got it? Got that
persons' face in front of you? Good. Now imagine that person wearing a mountain biking helmet. Now, keep going, he's coming towards
you on a single-track mountain bike trail riding a dual suspension
bike. There's just enough room for the two of you to pass comfortably
by each other. What do you do? What do you think is going to happen? It's an absolutely beautiful day. Everybody you've passed this
morning has commented on just that fact. Now this person who you
are most afraid of but you've never actually met makes eye contact
with you and says, "Good Morning, What a beautiful day." This bike
he's riding is just like one that you have thought about buying.
So...are you going to ask the devil how he likes his new ride? Then
you realize that you and the devil must have the same taste in mountain bikes. What does that tell you about him? What does that tell you
about you? Now imagine that the devil, or this person who you are
most afraid of is riding a bicycle exactly like one that you used to
have and that you thought was a piece of junk. Do you say anything
when he says hello, or do you blurt out, "Hey man I had a bike like
that and it was a piece of junk?" Let me say this again, "No messes or
foolish thinking are allowed out on the bike path." The answers to
these questions are just too obvious. Can you see why it is so, out on
the bike path? Would it be so hard not to always get off on the wrong
foot with everybody you meet in life who is just a little bit different
than you? You are, remember, to that person, just a little bit different
yourself, to them. Is that too much trouble for us to ask of ourselves,
to be considerate and work that into our definition about what being
civilized means?

What I guess I'm trying to convey, mainly about my own evolutionary understanding of my own personal spirituality, is that I feel like I have, in many ways, evolved. Today I talk about things I love and have a passion for. I don't spend a bunch of time thinking about fearful stuff or inventing it either. There are lots of people already doing that, and from what I see are doing a marvelous job at it. I used to be so incomplete, and I tried to fill the voids inside of me in ways that were harmful. That's what we do in our culture. That is what that blimp is saying that flies over the stadium crowd during football season. "Let me help with your pain, I can make you completely numb if you let me" is the message up there that lights up the night sky. The image you watch on your television set actually comes from their perspective, which includes more than a great vantage point from where to see a football field. You know what their message is. It's just like hundreds of messages we all get every day that tell us to disregard that most powerful part of ourselves and relinquish it to somebody who you don't even know, who promises you something that you've been fooled into thinking that you want. Because you do things you are not sure about, you put yourself on courses out to nowhere. Now, if you want to just go to nowhere and have a good time for a while, you need to do that. Life will take you there naturally anytime you want to go there and even when it's the last place you intended to go you can end up there very easily. In fact nowhere is the one place you can go that requires absolutely no effort to get to. For me, nowhere was the place I started from and where I realized that there was someplace else besides there. It is possible to find yourself in nowhere. Maybe that's its purpose. That is the real reason we all, all of us go there. We just don't need to stay there.

Out on the bike path is nowhere close to nowhere. There aren't even any signs to let you know how many miles away it is. Some theorize that it might even be impossible to get there from the bike path. From the bike path it's just as easy to get to the moon. To get away from nowhere and go straight to the moon, cover the whole trip, one hundred and twenty six thousand miles in a second. Be there that fast and be riding your mountain bike, leaving your tire tracks, yeah, leaving your tire tracks all over the place. Trying and making the greatest jumps then just hanging in the air of your imagination, twisting around and around, flipping end over end and landing perfectly on to a gentle downhill slope. Amazing, incredible, I'm so sure. But don't try me to try the moon. I've got no desire to go there. It looks just fine from right here. From right here I can do all I need to do to make myself happy. I finally learned that I live inside my own mind and my mind is connected to my soul. My soul is connected all through out and to the farthest points in space where lots of bike paths go.

What I am today is a person who's no longer searching for himself. I'm no longer trying to live up to other peoples' expectations of me either. What I'm doing here right now is what I believe I can do very well and I enjoy doing it. My hope of course is that you can somehow share my enjoyment of it. If I can bring joy into other peoples hearts just by being joyful in my own heart by this action you and I are now so intimately engaged, then I will never ever have to figure out again what it is that I need to do. We'll be doing it together. Won't that be fun?

Chapter 12

Nothing In A Box

🚲 🚲 🚲

T his is the way it works for me. It's not like falling off a log; it's not like that at all. I have actually experienced falling off a log while out mountain biking. When you mountain bike you encounter logs lying across the road all the time. You have to go over them if you're going to get very far down the trail, so getting over logs is not optional. Most people in the beginning just get off their bike and walk over the log pushing the bike. But, I'm sure you've guessed that at some point in the process of developing your biking skills, you are going to have to try to ride over or jump the log completely. It is a beautiful thing to watch an experienced mountain biker do a high bunny hop right over an obstacle. I can tell you too that reaching that kind of expertise is acquired only through hard work and practice. During the process of developing one's jumping skills you are almost guaranteed to do something exactly as easy as falling off a log and quite possibly up to and including the chance of breaking your silly neck. That is usually when most of us find out exactly just how easy it really is to fall off of a log. When they say, when someone describes something to you, and they attempt to convey to you a degree of difficulty a specific task may have attached to its completion or procedure, you can never be really sure if they know what it actually feels like themselves to really fall off a log.

I was coming down this hill one day headed to where I knew a large log blocked the trail. In the past I've always dismounted and walked my bike over the thing, got back on and went on my way. One of the mountain biking magazines I subscribe to had just run an article about how to jump over things on your bike. It had pictures and everything; I think they broke the jump into four separate moves. I studied it a while and practiced a little bit in front of my house. Practicing out in the cul-de-sac was not quite the same as a bike path and I knew I would have to find a place on a real trail if I was going to master this thing. A couple of days later I was in the woods and decided I was ready to at least try it. So I did. I crashed. It hurt. It was not easy at all to fall off that log. Well I should say it was easy falling, but it was not easy to fall and not get hurt too bad. I remember hanging there as my front wheel headed over the far side of the log. I can see it in my mind right now. I had all my weight going forward instead of back towards my rear tire.

This log was on a hill that was sloping downward toward the direction I was headed. This made the down angle even greater and the distance to the landing even farther. Forget the post-game analysis, Monday morning excuses and all that stuff. The deal is that I went over the handle bars and over my front end into the dirt into a forward roll down the hill sliding in the gravel on my aching back feeling like an idiot until I stopped completely, ending up looking at the sky through the tree branches. It was as easy as falling off a log. No, it takes practice to make falling off a log easy. I had not practiced at all up until this point on a real-world jump, so if you could have watched me do what I just described, easy would not be a word you would use to describe my fall. Stupid and idiotic looking would probably come into your mind first, then you might laugh, cringe or just shake your head and think to yourself, "What an idiot!" I did all those things as I stared up through the trees. Laughing hurt the most.

But back to how it works for me. It's not like falling off a log. Do you know how it feels to understand something for the first time? Maybe something you had to learn in school but it took forever for you to figure it out, but once you did you couldn't believe how stupid you were not to have not seen the solution right away. I mean, "it was right in front of you," isn't that what you said? That feeling is what I'm talking about here. It's a good example of the result, a feeling you experience that sometimes you get even when you weren't looking for it, that crazy euphoria, sometimes intense euphoria experienced in the sudden understanding and knowing of something once unknown.

I used to never talk about these kinds of things, feelings. I just didn't know how to or it just never occurred to me that they were things that needed to be talked about. Who would care about what I felt? In the beginning it was very difficult for me. It still is but I feel I need to do it anyway. Watching me learn to express myself was not a whole lot different from watching somebody crash their bike, you cringe a little right at first, shocked by the unexpected, then you are surprised and alarmed, you want to do something but you freeze up for a few moments not knowing what to do because the accident you're watching isn't yet over, it's still in motion and you can't do anything until the motion stops. Know in advance that there is nothing for you to do. But here goes.

Think for me about nothing in a box. Sometimes the only way for me to explain what it is and how it is I feel about things is to come from a place way far from where I need to go. That's just the way my brain works, it's the way my imagination begins and transforms into what I always hope will eventually turn out to be a pertinent conversation or observation. I usually start off with a crazy description and then ask some nutty question like, can you imagine nothing in a box? Struggling to find my way, I ask, can you imagine?   Then after I think I have your attention, I'm into it suggesting that you may need to, in order to understand where I want to go with this train of thought, maybe close your eyes while we do this, but that presents a problem in that you can't hear what I am saying here with your eyes closed. Yes, that was a not-too-subtle twist. What are we going to do? Okay, just for now go ahead and read what I'm writing here and try to remember it for later when it would be appropriate for you to be someplace with your eyes closed. One more time then, I want you to try to imagine nothing in a box. The size of the box is not important. At least the size of the box is not important to me. It may be very important to you. All I can tell you here is that because this box is only in your mind then how big it is won't matter, because for right now the only thing in the space of your imagination is this box and that space is supposed to be limitless. What kind of a box you imagine is not important either. Whatever kind of box you'd be comfortable with, a cardboard shoebox, a cigar box, the box your stereo came in, whatever. Begin to imagine the inside of the box. No, that's too easy. Let me tell you how all this came to me in the first place. It will put it into a perspective so maybe you can better understand. It'll put this void-filed box into perspective.

For weeks, months and years, I think since I had my first remote control television set and cable, like so many other people, I've had been changing the channels on the set like the station I was watching was on fire and the only way to put it out was to switch to another channel as fast as possible. I'd just watch, stare into the thing, have it on even when I wasn't watching it. It was, it had become, like a campfire to the Neanderthal I'd sometimes become when the thing was on. I had it set up so it was pointing right at me.

What did I expect? Up to seventy-something channels and still I could rarely find anything I felt was worth watching. I wondered if there was anything good out there in the world. All this time went by with me trying to find something worthwhile to watch on this thing. Then one day I just gave up and called up the cable company and said no more.

The big change for me, since I cut the cable cord, is that today I only have six channels and only three come in clear enough to watch. I can flip through them in about five seconds. I know right away that there is nothing on worth watching. Since I got rid of the cable there are so much more nothing that I get not to see. Today I can't imagine going back to that place where there was so much I couldn't watch. It takes a lot of our valuable time trying to choose about things so unimportant. Yes, there was always way too much nothing on. Today there is a lot less nothing going on in my life because I was able to see it for what it was and able to replace it with things more valuable. Things that I deem valuable, not things that other people say I should value, like for instance, cable television. People of the box were so quick to have an opinion. There were so many of them. Flipping through the channels, trying to decide which kind of box to imagine, all the things we engage ourselves in that do us absolutely no kind of good at all and sometimes harm us; (ever cringe at the sight of something you saw on television), things like our favorite addictions, no matter what they are, all, together, they act like huge barriers that keep us from getting down to the business of simply being a human beings. What do you see in your box?

Maybe what you should do is to look at it this way. Do what I did. Sit down in your favorite chair and just stare at the TV. Get real comfortable. Then just begin to watch the television screen. Easy, you've done this before. Can you see yourself there now as I set this picture of you up in your mind? There you are, maybe in your favorite recliner, feet uplifted thusly, maybe a cold beverage at your side. Aw, doesn't that feel good, just relaxing and watching the tube? Maybe the cold drink in one hand and the remote in the other, channel surfing going through the seventy-five or so channels of wondrous color on the big screen? What time is it? When do you start your watching exercises?

How long can you go? What's the longest period of time you've spent watching TV, what's your record? Do you remember what you watched? Do you remember what was on last night, last weekend? How many hours did you work in relation to hours watching TV, to sleeping? Don't misunderstand; I don't have a problem with people who watch a lot of TV. It keeps the traffic down on the bike paths. But are you yourself, with that beverage and a sack of paper-wrapped food by your side doing maybe too much of a good thing?

Now, back to your imagination. Try this for me. Now that I've set a scene for you (or it could be for anybody, don't take it personally), but instead of imagining yourself over there on the couch, think of yourself as a spirit, separate from your physical body. Think of yourself, your spiritual self, as a transparent shadow of yourself. Think now of yourself as a fast forming stream of electrons moving through the air, off the couch, down from the recliner moving through the air, sailing around your great room, circling the ceiling fan a few times, then as sharp as a needle headed straight into the center of your television screen. Now that's getting off the couch! Right into the screen, there you go and there you are on the inside looking out back into the room. At the same time you are still over there on the couch with the remote in your hand. The you over there on the couch can't see you there in the box looking out at yourself. He has no idea as to what just happened. He's going to just sit there like he always does getting up every once in a while to got to the bathroom and maybe get another beverage. He's been switching the channels a lot faster since he quit smoking a few months ago. He's put on a few pounds too, you notice. He works awfully hard but nobody appreciates him much. Some days he looks like a rat in a trap out there in the world. Rat traps, maybe that's a good analogy? What would we design if we wanted to catch ourselves? What if we became a menace in some people's eyes and they wanted to rid the world of us? Wouldn't it be a good idea if they could get us all in one place and exterminate us all in one fell swoop? What if we found out sometime in the future that we were made to live forever but constant exposure to remote controls shortens our lives dramatically? That's pretty crazy thinking, made to live forever, people thinking we were bad enough to think up diabolical plans to shorten our life spans and then limit our ability to control our destiny? Who out there in the world would ever think that we were bad? Never mind. But look, keep looking out from the inside of the set out to you over there in the cushy chair. He looks pretty bored to me and it's just going to be a few minutes until he gets so bored with us, you and I inside this television set, that he's going to turn the sound off, hit the mute button and start listening to the stereo. The music will get louder and louder and he will drink a few more beverages until he gets hungry. Then he'll get himself something to eat, turn off the music and turn the sound back on to the television set, and fall asleep with us watching him. He's so blasted that he doesn't even know we're here having to sit through all this stuff with him. It makes me mad, so much nothing in that box he's in.

That's what I used to see from my box. That was the channel that one day made me change. That was the channel that, once I was able to see it for what it was, a big fat mess, that moved me finally off that target range for everything I had let shoot at me from the outside world with that electron gun. Man, I was a sitting duck! I was helpless. Think about it, I was even paying them fifty dollars a month for the privilege of being a target for them. I took some hits.

What do you see from your box? I hope you get better reception than I used to have. The channel I needed to watch the most didn't even come into my house. No matter how many times I'd cycle through the channels I could not find it. I did not realize that it was me. That I was the channel I was looking for. The one channel that didn't even require anything more than what I was born with. Part of which was the simple ability to place myself in a position to view what I was doing from a new perspective, like from the inside of a box.

I found something for myself in that nothingness in a box. I found this kid who was me, the real me. It took some work but I was not alone. That's what I learned. I had never been alone and there was nothing I needed to be made to fear. Me, I was led to a mountain bike. I don't know how it happened, but one thing that allowed it to happen was for me to realize just how constrained I was connected to boxes and ideas that didn't make sense to me anymore. A way of living that caused me to hurt myself unnecessarily. I thought I was connected to the world but I wasn't. I was connected to an idea that was somebody else's. No more, not since I became able to recognize for myself so much nothing quickly in so many boxes. They're everywhere. These days I can't even imagine myself inside that box looking out at me. I'm not there anymore. The couch is empty most of the time. The earth is filled with too much possibility to use just one point to view it from.

My recommendation is to trade some of your couch time for something about you, something that might put you on a better path to whom you might really be or if you already are that person move that to another level. Choose at least some of the time the place on the remote that causes the television to go dark and quiet. My television doesn't say either on or off. It just has a button with the word "Power" printed under it. That's the button that turns my TV on. It also works to make the thing not work.

The bike path is my way for right now. That doesn't mean it has to be yours. It's my place to feel the wind and my power to move through it. It's my place to feel myself moving and where I can let that being move me in ways I had forgotten about. I can see myself there anytime from here, in motion, flying forward like imagination mixing with the forest, merging with the air, running into light, becoming change itself, turning into the feelings, not knowing fear.

Just in telling you about me allows me to see more of myself somehow. The inside of me is so much more important than the outside, it is constant, eternal, and so it is with all of us I believe. Why that fact gets forgotten at times is for some of us a great mystery; then, at those times, we're just incapable to see what problems that this kind of separation from even our own selves can create. So many things try so hard to be influential on our outward appearance and all the things that frame our modern being. So too our spiritual selves are deluged by those who only need us to make them seem more power-ful. We enter into a kind of a race that has no specific end, just a promise of improved enjoyment if we continue to race. We get caught up in the race; it's exciting some times. It's as if all there was is this huge ego in a constant state of recruitment to make us all just like it, unappeasable, always hungry for something more, inadequate by design, needing us only to reassure it of its supremacy, always quick to change direction on us as its wants change without reason. It is there only to be fed by our own feeding frenzies that can cause us to devour each other for its sadistic pleasure, surrendering in our hunger to please, our need for its approval. We're then unable to recognize what's happening while we're in its grasp; we've forgotten for a time that the inside of us is constant and not really dependent on it at all. Yet we become so mixed and missed, lost in all the background noise of that common back grounding super ego-driven existence its created just for us. Gladly we offer up our praise to its command. We've stayed too late too often at its all night bashes. Then we discover too late that it takes a lot to separate from a beast who's used to having its teeth at our throat. Who exists only to drink our blood.

Just thinking about changing our thinking scares us to death. If all you know is someone hitting you over the head with a hammer all your life, you might be afraid were it to stop. It might take you a while to realize that life without the hammer might possibly be better than life as how it has always been for you. But wait, take heart, I'm here to say that I believe the road to peace and clarity is built into you, it's hard wired. It has always been there. You can live beyond the reach of the beast. You know yourself that you used to have it, but you lost it. No, not really, you just misplaced it. I think all you have to do is look for it, seek it out. I think we spend a bunch of time during our lifetime looking for things in wrong places. We think great things have to be hard to obtain and require years of study and toil to attain some sort of perfect state of existence. Just like me, you may have once forgotten that you had it with you all the time. You just needed something to happen to you so you could be reminded, to be in some way alone and quiet, calm without the need to turn to anybody except yourself, or just really feel that way, so as to allow a natural part of your condition to come into your consciousness and then be able to experience a form of transcendence or inward transformation of your being and finally understand it. I hope it's happened to you already, and you are more than what you used to be. I hope you never again become so wrapped up in things so unimportant. Learning and understanding may take some work, much changing, rearranging your priorities and totally reevaluating your sense of values, at least those things and more. Go slow and rediscover yourself. Take a look in there for your self, your soul. It's there; it's just under a bunch of junk. Junk that needs to be examined carefully before it's thrown out. Not because there is any question about it being trash, but because part of this process is to be able to recognize this stuff for what it is. Take your time. Get it done. When finally this box is empty and all it contained has been dealt with and if need be discarded, you can get rid of the box too. There's nothing in it. It's empty.

Now, how to get rid of this empty box, this box full of nothing. I don't know about you, but I'm not going to worry about it. That's not my job anymore. My job was just to bring it to your attention and suggest just how really empty it always was. I'm headed down the bike path. I'm not looking in the box and nothing in the box is looking out at me. I am clear and free, moving down my favorite trails, going right to go left, up to go down, hearing my tires hum over the bike path, feeling my front shock compress and expand as I negotiate these rocks, bounce over this log, duck my head under these branches, lock my brakes and slide my rear tire around this downhill hairpin curve. I feel the power my body creates propelling me up this mountain trail to its summit where I can see beyond forever. And I know beyond forever when I see it, I feel its wind, the taste of its special vibration in the center of my being, always with me, keeping me centered and raising me up, carrying me along its winding wondrous path. Seeing forward and looking backward at the same time I'm able to myself understand the importance of some things and the insignificance of others. This morning as my bike flew lightly over a small log that had fallen across the trail, that had been place there just for me, for my pleasure by last night's thunderstorm, I thought about you and this message you are reading here, how I wanted to leave it with you; and as I touched down back to earth I fell right through the bike path and was suddenly in a land of complete contentment, surrounded by the natural world's simple beauty. The new trail led out into a piece of light reflected off a leaf. My wheels rolled easily into some inner space where I felt cradled by some overwhelming sense of contentment and I seemed to be floating above the world. Then, there was the box just below me coming slowly apart into its six equal parts. Each part began to fall away from every other part, slowly spinning end over end, twirling like a spiral galaxy in infinite space, growing smaller and smaller as each part dissolved completely, taken away by an unfelt invisible wind. I watched this and as I watched it, I knew that you and I would be okay, now, without the box.

Man, did I just jump that log or what?

Chapter 13

Being Lost

🚲 🚲 🚲

A Reply

You're right about being in the woods and being in decent shape (it's been over two years since I've had a cigarette and about a year and a half since I put down the beer) but alas, contrary to your belief, I've not done too well in the business world here of late. Reinventing myself included confronting my OCD attitude about business and what all that was doing to me. Right now I'm just trying to learn a new way of life, hopefully one that can improve my financial situation and at the same time "fit" in a way that won't kill me.

The good news is that being poor isn't all that bad and I think it's just a place where I needed to be while I configured the plan for the

rest of my life. I'm pretty excited about it. Other news is that I found
a thread to follow with my mountain biking experiences where I
believe I can contribute something really important. I found this place
in my heart, got rid of a bunch of fear and pretty much just let the
spiritual side of myself go where it wanted to. I just sit on my mountain bike and let things take form. Yesterday I was out on the trail
and because it was so wet, I guess from all the rain this week, coupled
with a major amount of freshly fallen leaves, this trail I've ridden hundreds of times in the past looked so different that, just for a moment, I
had the thought that I was lost. I had this flash that I was someplace
where I'd never been before. Just as fast I knew I wasn't lost at all
and the feeling of being lost got replaced with the recognition of just
how remarkable this place called the bike path is. It is different every
day. I'm different every day and yesterday I thought about that as I
rode, these differences and being lost in them.

I thought about the idea of being lost and what all that meant.
Then, as I rode along it occurred to me. It occurred to me in such a
way that I had to stop and just get off of my mountain bike and just
stand there and savor the moment of discovery, there in the middle of
the woods, about being lost.

I'd been lost before. All of us have experienced a situation where,
say you were going somewhere unfamiliar and you thought you knew
where you were, but then all of a sudden, at some point you realized
you didn't know where you were at all and you had to admit that to
yourself. That place where you made that admittance is the place we
all think of as "lost." But that's not the thought that stopped me in my
tracks. What occurred to me is that the realization of being lost ends
the dilemma of being lost. In other words, at the exact instant you
realize you're lost, you're not anymore. Lost is a real place. It's the
point where from then on you have a very real direction and understanding as to where you are headed, away from lost. You're then free
to be on your way to wherever it was you were going. Only difference
is you are just having to start from somewhere besides the sense of
knowing you were having until you were lost. The only time then you

were really lost was the time when you thought you knew where you were but you didn't, you only thought you knew. You were wrong then, you were really lost then, you just didn't know it.

Being lost is a place. It's a kind of shift in our understanding of where we are whether it is out on the bike path or somewhere in the universe. When we lose all our points of known reference or those points have changed in a way that we no longer can recognize them, then we are in danger of standing on the doorstep to that place called lost which is much more dangerous than actually being there.

We're taught that being lost is not a good thing. "Be careful, don't get lost out there." I notice that there is never a shortage of people "out there" that are always trying to confuse us about this natural state of being. Telling us it's a place to be feared, being lost, talking to us like we're lost at the very time that they are talking about it. Holding books up in the air that they say have all the answers. Some of the books have their pictures on the front and some of the books come with videos and their pictures are on the back cover, too. Some of the books are free, some aren't. I don't know. All I want to do is to put enough words down on paper to make up one of these things called books that I too can hold up in the air and put my picture on the back of and maybe not have to give away. That will become a state of being for me that won't be anything like being lost and I think I could do that for the rest of my life. I think I can do it for the rest of my life because I love what I'm doing right now and I'm in love with loving it. Understand, this activity, mountain biking, does not replace or take away from my relationships with other people who I love, it only makes those relationship better, stronger more deeply felt. This sense of getting away and thinking about these things, to some so insignificant, is so wonderful that when I'm back in the world my mind is able to sort the important somehow better from the not so, I'm able, I believe to distinguish better the real from the unreal no matter who is holding whatever up in the air at whatever moment in time throughout the day. At least I hope so. I'm just riding along now having fun and everyday finding such incredible things in my path as I go.

Chapter 14

Biking Around
The Cul-De-Sac

🚲 🚲 🚲

ast evening I looked up at the moon. It was just a sliver, the
phase where it's sometimes called God's fingernail, barley
there at all, above the western horizon watching and waiting,
like me, for the last of the daylight to be pulled down into darkness. It
was beautiful, the sun setting and the moon rising at the same time. I
could easily make out Venus just below and to the left of the new
moon, so close I could imagine myself just reaching up and touching
it. The sky was so especially blue there; contrasted by the amber gold
rays of the sun and the smoky dark clouds that framed the whole of
the western sky like a cosmic picture frame. Broad white streaks of

sunlight radiated thickly from their invisible source below the horizon up through a thin layer of fine pink clouds; and as I sat there still on my mountain bike in the middle of the cul-de-sac in front of my house, there were no more questions that needed a reply, all the urgency of day was simply and completely neutralized. I thought to myself about how this wonderful show was on every evening. I thought about how available it was to all of us. I thought about how poets and writers had by the thousands for all recorded time tried to put this simple beauty into words, how artists have tried to paint it, photograph it, replicate it somehow, all of us, all humanity being moved so powerfully by the simple beauty of the setting sun.

My neighbors around the cul-de-sac think I'm a little weird. That's not just conjecture on my part, they've told me so. That doesn't mean that they don't like me but most people still have trouble accepting the fact that some of us can earn a living in a way that doesn't include getting up in the morning and driving downtown to sit in front of a desk all day. They accept it, but even so, have trouble equating the ability to actually earn a living in another way different from what they're familiar with. Earn a living, now there's a concept. How do you earn a living? It sounds a lot like, how do you justify your existence? Sometimes I think I can hear them thinking, "All we ever see you do is ride that stupid bike around and around in the cul-de-sac," and "I don't know what he's doing. It looks like he's just staring up at the sky, and look, our cat's out there with him. He's doing the same thing. What a nut!"

My neighbors always seem unsatisfied with my explanations as to how I earn a living; they repeatedly ask me for better explanations as to what exactly I do. I tell them the truth, I'm in the computer software business and I write stories about mountain biking. I explain that I have about as much luck with one as I do the other sometimes, but then, every once in a while, I get lucky.

Nothing is for sure. It never was. Even when I got up and drove to an office every day like they do now, that too was never a sure thing, but I guess it was a lot easier to pretend it was when everybody around you is pretending too. It's just the best answer I can give. I don't know how to explain it. I don't know how to explain to them where these things I write about come from. Finding things to write about is what I do. How does anybody explain that? Some days I end up completely off my target and end up writing a story about just riding my bike in my cul-de-sac. I ride over forty miles a week out on the trails plus maybe another five around my neighborhood. For me, now, circling the cul-de-sac is like taking a smoke break during the day and like a few beers with my work buddies when I used to wear the suit and go to that thing called an office five days a week. That's not even close to where I am now.

Today, I'm right here, me and the neighbor's cat, watching the sun go down and the moon come up. The cat and I, both of us know, that's the important stuff. When things like that are going on all at once I'm as totally involved as a brain surgeon. I'm in to it. I'm not just watching either, I'm part of the whole thing up there. I'm as important to the event as the event is to me. We exist together, interdependent with each other, tied to a daily definable measurable onward cadence in time and space, destined to become transfixed at sundown, moonrise, circle the cul-de-sac time. Automatically we've all followed our unseen vectors all day long just to be right here when the cat and I and whoever else comes around to line up like commuters, ready to board in predetermined sequence our next vehicle of conveyance, albeit now, just in the mind, to this peace at the end of the day. All I know is that I love this time I spend doing what other people describe as 'nothing' when they see me doing it. They just don't yet understand, nothing is really something.

I get singled out all the time but there are three or four three- or four-year-olds who also live on my street and spend time with me doing nothing. They don't seem to need an explanation. Petting my dog and picking zinnias are a big deal for small people. Me too. I've enjoyed it here lately watching these kids go from tricycle to bicycle with training wheels to without the training wheels. Another cul-de-sac neighbor has a nine-month-old daughter who has just learned to point up to the sunset and say, "sun." Last night she said, "moon" for the first time. Tonight she pointed up and saw both the moon and the sun at the same time, "moon, sun," she says. Only nine months old, she points at me and says, "bike." I look at the cat. The cat looks at me. We know what's next. "Cat."

The cat and I, we know we have another convert here who will see the world with clarity for a time. Together, all of us look to the celestial events going on in front and above us. I think of all the wonder all around us. This is really something here tonight, I smile inside to myself. The cat looks over in my direction and I nod back my agreement, Yeah, and the night is just getting started."

Venus is that much closer to my hand.

Chapter 15
My Snake Story

It occurred to me the other day, while out on the bike path, that I'd
not seen as many snakes this spring as I did last year. I had
chalked it up to the fact that I've been getting out much earlier
this spring and was usually finished with my daily ride about the same
time I used to begin. Back then it seemed that I'd come up on one rep-
tile or another about every third ride or about once a week during the
spring and before their routine changed. I'd read that snakes become
nocturnal in the hotter months up until September or October.

It had just been a long time since I'd spent so much time in the
woods and my snake type classification skills were pretty rusty so I

bought myself the "Field Guide to Reptiles and Amphibians" pub-
lished by the National Audubon Society. It's a great book, lots of
color photos and habitat descriptions. Pretty soon, with the help of
this book I was identifying garter snakes, rat snakes, pig snakes and
even a king snake. Pretty cool stuff and recognizing and determining
quickly that a snake is of the non-poisonous variety takes all the stress
out of the encounter. Of course this is not what this chapter is about.

Yesterday, I was doing the loop, having started from the south
trailhead and was having another fantastic ride, moving swiftly
through the forest down by a place known as Tranquility Park.
There's a place in the trail there, you may know it, where the sun
shines brightly down on the trail right by a remote control car course
and where they're now building a new BMX track. I'm headed downhill when I see in front of me something that I know right a way is
not a tree root, its right in front of me, it's a snake, it's a big snake, it's
facing me, it's a rattlesnake, I can't stop in time, I can't chance running over it, the trail's too narrow, I can't go around. I could have
rolled over it, but that didn't occur to me fast enough. All I can do is
brake as hard as I can and lay the bike down fast. This is a Ra-Ra-
RA-RATTLESNAKE! My bike tires bite the dirt and I'm right
behind them going face down across the trail, face five inches off the
trail and frozen, sliding in, finally, to a complete stop. I freeze. I think
that's what you're suppose to do when your nose is about three feet
away from the nose of a pit viper.

I tell you, there are moments in all our lives that stand out,
become etched in our memory. This morning, a freak combination of
timing had put me and a rattlesnake in each other's definition of
harm's way. We all know and accept that there are always inherent
dangers in mountain biking, or for that matter, just walking the trails.
If you bike very much you can become sometimes oblivious to those
dangers or you can remain respectful but statistically pretty certain
that the odds of ending up in such an event is pretty remote. "Now,
turn if you will, to my file on rattlesnakes, new entry: See picture of
me with deadly snake. I used to always call this part of the bike path

Florida because of the sunlight. From now on it's 'Rattlesnake Alley'(notation recorded brain file cabinet 6-27-02)."

Thank goodness it was still early in the day, about 7:50 AM, a little bit later in the day and this guy would be a bit more awake and probably not so docile and understanding to guys so close up and personal. After a few more seconds of total stillness and silence I moved slowly backwards like a snake myself, crawling backwards over my fallen bike, putting safe distance between my exposed nose and the seemingly docile and (thankfully) cold blooded reptilian. Thank you, Lord!

I guess the point of me wanting to share this bit of personal bike experience is that it serves as a good reminder that we all need to be mindful at all times of what we're doing and where we are out there on the bike path. Times of the year, traffic, weather and trail conditions greatly differ, sometimes day to day, and all should play a part in how we approach our day's ride. Just don't forget about snakes this time of year. Speaking of snakes, I need to finish this story.

After I'd regained my composure and reclaimed my bike from the easy reach of the snake, I decided to give the rattler a wide berth and walked up to try and bypass this section of trail we all now refer to as "Rattlesnake Alley." Two park workmen were just arriving to begin their day working on the aforementioned BMX track addition. To them I shared my experience and cautioned them of the nearness of the rattlesnake to where they were working. In doing so I also mentioned that probably there were some rules of the park concerning the protection of all wildlife within its boundaries and the snake itself was guilty of nothing but being a rattlesnake. They, of course, as park personnel fully agreed, then one of them got a shovel and we all went down the hill, found it, and the guy with the shovel cut its head off.

You have a choice here to decide for yourself if this ending is happy or not. They gave me the rattle. I attached it to the front of my bike. I think it looks better than the manufacturer's logo. I'm sure the snake would disagree. I don't know. All I do know is that I love mountain biking. Every day is an adventure.

Chapter 16

The Trail Ride To Transhumanism

I've been doing a bit of research on the subject of genetics, especially the theoretical side of what I'm sure will become an even larger political football than it is already. Monkeying around with the human genome is to some the epitome of blasphemy. To others, some whom now are defining themselves as "Transhumanists," believe that in the future a genetically designed human species is the way to eliminate, once and for all, unhealthy weaknesses inherent to the human condition. The Transhumanists theorize that within 100 years (some say 50), scientists will be able to develop a human being so well designed genetically that it (he or she) will be completely free of all life-threatening diseases like cancer, diabetes, cardiac artery disease etc. Further, they point out in their theory that in the past, or at least going back to modern man's ancestor Australopithecus Africanus (about 2 million years ago), the archeological evidence suggests that higher human intelligence may be simply attributable to physical brain size. If, while mixing up this better recipe for a person, they theorize, you throw in some genetically constructed DNA with larger brain size attributes included, you might be able to produce a human with a brain twice as large as yours or mine. The jump looks like this: Australopithecus, around 800 cubic centimeters; Homo Sapiens, 2200cc; and this new specimen, 4400cc. The theory goes on to surmise that this new "super human" might be smart enough philosophically, intelligently and spiritually to figure out a way to eliminate social problems like war and other catastrophic human endeavors. Think about it, a future free of disease and war! The human lifespan increased dramatically!

To some it sounds too much like heaven and you can't be here on earth and in heaven at the same time. You need to suffer. "If God wanted you to do smart things he would of created you that way. So shut up and hand me the torch, there's witches we need to be burning."

For me, I'm pretty basic; I just try, like they say, to keep the rubber side down and the plastic side up. I'm completely content riding my old bike until it wears completely out. I guess I'm kind of a throwback that way. I don't see the need right now to alter my pretty well dug in style of path riding. That is not to say that I don't have a great appreciation for those of you who feel they need to push the proverbial envelope sometimes. I just think there's room for both philosophical approaches within the sport of mountain biking.

These days it's hard not to notice the quickly evolving designs of these machines we love so much. I call them "flying bicycles". I think they're great. Most of us remember back when we were kids (this morning for some of us) and making jumps from shoveled up dirt and constructing dangerous transverses from leftover construction materials like concrete blocks and two-by-ten yellow pine framing boards. I still remember picking myself up after a particularly spectacular crash and the sinking feeling realization of a rear tire rim too twisted to ever turn freely again. We were like scientists pushing the envelope. Every once in a while we'd fly like the Wright Brothers and some days the sand mixed with the red clay of Georgia produced colorful riveting tattoos upon us, by-products of these, our spectacular failures. No hat, no shirt, no sense, but the desire to fly.

Fifty years from now when they're going through the pantry looking for the ingredients for this Transhuman dude, I hope they don't forget the portion that instills in us the need to fly sometimes. For me, every time I pull up on my handlebars to better transverse a fallen log or a dried streambed, I can't help but think sometimes about the pictures you see on the covers of just about every mountain biking magazine out there. Some think this choice of art overplays the reality of the activity. The flying bicycles dominate the cover art for this industry. At first, when I'd see these displays of extreme machines flying, my mind would ask itself things like, "does anybody care anymore about us guys who spend most of their time riding our mountain bikes here on planet earth? What is the deal here, what's the draw about jumping off a mountain?" I fully expect to see a new bike soon with twenty-two feet of travel in the front shock and eighteen in the back.

There is this wonderful feeling I get every time I ride my own mountain bike. Flying is the best word I know that describes it. Not off the ground so much like the cover art stuff, but flying just the same. My spirit takes off too. Altitude is not a measurement of the distance between my tires and the bike path while I'm riding. My personal altitude is the "out there" beyond the physical world and the Newtonian laws that confine. While I'm on the bike path I'm at play with the whole space-time continuum. I'm bound by no laws to interrupt my thoughts. As I travel deeper into the forest I'm traveling deeper into what makes up my thoughts, my life, my soul and all connectedness to the universe beyond.

Yeah, flying bicycles, a good idea for cover art. So far I guess it's the best thing the photographers can come up with to describe this simple and at the same time beautiful sensation attached to our wondrous activity of mountain biking. The thing to remember I suppose is that there is a spirit up there flying in the air along with the biker and the bike. I don't have a camera that will take a picture of a spirit. I just have these words. I hope they will suffice until the Transhuman guy comes along.

Chapter 17

Path Work

🚲 🚲 🚲

For a long time all I did was take from the mountain. Then one day I decided I needed to put something back into something I was getting so much from. The best avenue for that payback was to simply join my local mountain bike club and volunteer my help in the ongoing work of trail maintenance. I came to believe that the trails, its riders and the mountain itself, all were connected in some special way. In doing, I discovered that there is much about the work of bike trail maintenance that appeals to me. Riding the trails so much that they need to be specially and regularly maintained is certainly an obvious pleasure. That is my favorite part of the whole process; my riding helps contribute to the trails need for maintenance. It's nice to feel needed.

It should be a given that mountain bike trails need to be maintained or there would be no trails. A thing as narrow as a three-foot wide dirt mountain bike path would on its own cease to exist rather quickly without the traffic it was designed for in the first place. But without proper maintenance, that small way through the forest would degrade and become almost impossible to travel over time as weathering and changing riding patterns combine to distort its route. Rain and temperature erode earth away where there is no plant life rather quickly. Without proper maintaining by people who care and know what they are doing, the dirt path would quickly turn to a rock path and become very difficult to ride in places. At that point riders would be forced to blaze new trail next to existing old trail in order to just be able to ride. We've all seen this evidence; a place in the path that after a rainy week becomes too muddy to pedal through and we see harder ground next to it and turn on to it in order to maintain momentum and safe traction through what weather had turned into a mud river. Then, that muddy quagmire quickly becomes a rock garden as the top surface of soil is, over time, completely washed away.

Besides adding a bit of uncontrolled danger, all of us understand that riding over and into and through a muddy trail is detrimental to the trail. Some days in some conditions it's just impossible to avoid these kinds of places—you have no choice but to splash and ooze your way along, venturing on the edge of control. For me, riding in those kinds of conditions can be a blast of fun; I love the sound my tires make as they sink into the gooey stuff, squishing out a kind of music, punctuating my ride with extra sensations. The muddy spray gets all over you, covering your legs and back, all of you, and your bike ends up with this coating of finely brewed mud that is applied like artistic brush stokes by a master painter. The muddy earth mixed sometimes with pine straw and rotting leaves creates a special paint that only enhances for me the appearance of an already beautiful instrument. This thing, my bike, was intended to wear this layer of

authenticity, this flying mud. At the end of a day's ride, when you
return to the trailhead and your car, you can feel the eyes of other
adventurers admire the muddy paint job you've spent the last couple
of hours applying with the utmost care and concentration. Then, as
you dismount your bike there and step away after attaching it to your
vehicle for the ride back home, can you only then get a chance to
admire your artwork and to really appreciate this artistic image of
beauty it has become, its quality, this picture of fun covered with the
trail itself, a vivid snapshot of an example of a kind of cosmic connectedness, the spirit of the bike merged with the spirit of the living trail.
It's your own special creation.

Part of appeal of the sport of mountain biking is that basic connection to the natural forest. The single-track leads you through a
beautiful world and not just the physical world. For me it has the
power to be both physical and spiritual at the same time. When I'm
thinking in this dualistic mode I feel as though I'm in a holy place.
The bike path is my church. Trail work is my tithing to its grandeur.
Its mud is my baptismal; my trail work is my meager offering in
return for so much I receive, so freely given.

Just like the activity of mountain biking awoke senses in me I had
somehow misplaced for a while, trail work illuminated other areas
into my consciousness. Doing path work may be opening other for-
merly long undisturbed windows into my self. It may release thoughts
that were dear but misplaced, giving me new opportunity to discover
more about my true self. I can imagine so much and so much more
can be imagined if accompanied by meaningful experience. Trail work
provides this door to this additional opportunity. More can be moved
out there than earth and rocks.

I missed the last bike club meeting because I had to travel out of
town but I got an email saying that a workday for the coming Sunday
morning was scheduled. This would be my second experience as a
member of a trail maintenance crew and I was looking forward to it.
It was a thirty-degree wind-blown January morning. What others
and I were about to do was more about mountain biking than any-

thing you'd ever read in one of those mountain biking magazines with
a picture of a flying bicycle on the cover. What was going on here this
frosty morning was the gathering of people who, for whatever reason,
had come to the mountain one day and like me, had received a wonderful gift. This morning, and many mornings in the past and to be
many in the future, the able, the giving and the concerned were about
to contribute their time and energy to make sure this special place
would continue. But more than just their time and energy, they were
returning something that usually goes unspoken, something that you
can't put a value on or complicate with bureaucracy and definitions,
something that just appears in the doing of the good deed, different
for all who partake of the experience but every bit as meaningful to
all. A portion of each person's individual being was being bestowed
directly back to the source where a special connection had been made
and the impulse to be here in this activity could not be resisted.

This morning, out here on the bike path, on the surface, we
looked like gardeners working the ground, heads bowed and backs
bent into the labor of trail work. I can only relate to you what goes on
in my mind while doing this kind of activity. Some would say not
much. Others might just see more. Out on the bike path there is room
for all and as I've found out there are extra shovels if you're interested. Think about it; if you're the type of person who enjoys a little mud
on your mountain bike, consider that there is a whole mountain of it
out there waiting for your enjoyment.

This morning was most enjoyable. I can only tell of a small part of
it because I was only a small part myself. That kind of simplicity was
pleasurable as I didn't have to make one single decision on my own.
It's nice sometimes to allow someone else to judge your abilities from
a totally different perspective than what you're accustomed. You simply ask the work leader, "What can I do?" If you think about it, its
almost magical; up until the instant of his answer you've always
defined yourself as completely different from what you are about to
become. Your question is considered for about two seconds as you are
also visually sized up as to physical ability for varying tasks. "We

need rocks, big rocks found and brought over here, then with this sledge hammer, some of them need to be broken up and put onto the clay surface we're laying here." How wonderful, directions even I could understand. And look! Right here next to the trail, a whole bunch of big rocks! Today is my lucky day! This was different than shoveling mud and pushing a wheelbarrow like the last time I volunteered to work. I'm diversifying! But hey, either job was more fun than my usual routine. That thought alone produce an enthusiasm in me most enjoyable. I savored it and as I went about un-wedging great rocks from the earth and transporting them back a few feet up to the path, my mind wandered in completely new directions.

The area of track we were working led uphill from where we were to the very top of the mountain. We were about a mile ride away from it. From where I was working I could see about an eighth of a mile until the trail meandered off to the north and upward and out of sight. It occurred to me how the grade of this section of mountain path was similar to that of the great pyramids of Cheops in Egypt. In my mind I was transported back thousands of years and became a worker at that ancient site. I imagined the great pyramid of Khufu at Giza and the great Sphinx and how remarkable they were to all. What homage as a stone mover I was paying now to the work of ancients with similar job descriptions. I hefted another heavy limestone rock and I felt that kind of connection as my pile of rocks grew longer and wider next to the construction area. Inside I was beaming with pride as the evidence of my work increased along in time. This morning, right here on the side of this great mountain, I had become a moving part of a machine, that with its other parts and their efforts, were changing visibly the area here today. Many wheelbarrows of wonderful sturdy clay passed me to higher ground being pushed by other similarly inspired devotes. We were an order within a larger universe of practitioners now actively engaged in our giving of alms. With each strike of my sledgehammer I connected further with a timeless brotherhood dedicated to the greater intentions of being human. I'm not overstating this at all. This is what trail work is.

I felt it. I could see the change. New shapes were appearing all over the trail. I could feel the connectedness of other humans working together on a common goal. I was truly part of a group and I felt I belonged. It was fluid, it had direction and its accomplishment was never in question. We all understood that the task at hand would never be completed, that more rains would come one day and wash even this work away, but what was going on was so necessary to the holding on to something so special. It was and would always be a never-ending process. What a wonderful thought, a never-ending process. Unseen forces were at work even now as we patched and improved the living trail. Forces unseen at work to create even better areas of mud to slide through, fallen trees to jump over and discover new launches from where my spirit might next take flight.

Off the bike path we always have to describe ourselves, tell who we are to people whom we don't know, in a way that sometimes makes us out to be more or less than what we really are. Our lives are complicated. I read recently that if it takes you more than fifteen words to describe what you do, you really don't know what you do. It's nice to have a weekend morning from time to time when we can be so much less than what we are and at the same time be so much more. I'm very proud of my description. I'm a rock mover.

Chapter 18

Evaporation

🚲 🚲 🚲

Why some of us have to try to explore the entire universe of knowledge and some of us need only to look out our kitchen window to find a spiritual connection to real knowing doesn't have to be a mystery. It's okay, but not always necessary to bequeath and endow great fortunes on research into the scientific and philosophical exploration of the human mind and its inner workings. Maybe it's that just the search for proofs in itself is proof enough that there is something more than the obvious at work in our lives. The act of human searching is something we can't help, something we're born with and its innate demanding need for an object to be searched for is, I believe, a vital characteristic of our species, one of many that shape us, define us and cause us to always strive for things beyond our reach. I believe that wherever one is, no matter where that may be, a place real or imagined, a place where your being exists at a point in space and a place in time is always just a simple shift in ones mindset away to a completely new dimension of experience. Look right, look left, look up then close your eyes and breathe. It happened into my mind again this morning.

The weather here the last couple of weeks has been dismal. It's the time of the year when the force of the wind is strong and consistent enough to keep the set of wind chimes outside my screened porch lightly clanging almost continually. The sun just can't quite seem to make it through this constant cover of clouds. The rain, though not heavy at all, just seems to hang about, somehow not at all sure of itself, as if it can't decide what it wants to do. It was a week ago today since I was out on the bike path. On that morning my tires sank into a trail turned to mud and I knew that my fun was not good for the mountain. So, here I am, waiting for this malaise of moisture and wind to evaporate.

What's going on out there on the mountain is important to the mountain. I know that. It's telling me very clearly that it would simply like to have some time to itself for a couple of weeks. Yeah, the mountain speaks to me. It always has. There was a time when I didn't choose to hear what the mountain was trying to tell me, or anybody else, including my soul. I just plowed along in the mud of my day angry at things that were beyond my control. There were all theses unread messages full of communications written in bad penmanship, scrawled on little pink squares of paper that were being stuffed into my metaphysical mailbox by invisible hands. My computer mailbox too was replete with too many individual wants that greeted me each day like a nest full of baby birds that needed their morning feeding. They needed constant feeding. I paid mindless attention to them. I paid little attention to anything but the desires of my own ego. Even today it tries to embroil me. It is tenacious for sure, but like in a play where the villain's mask is

111

finally removed, I can see it for what it is and what it is not. What it used to be was that great barrier to my true life objectives. My true self was like the mountain in winter, I had my own canopy of cloudiness not allowing even the smallest rays of sunshine to reach the ground or into my heart. There are so many things that have so many misunderstood purposes. I didn't even know that I was overwhelmed.

At some point in time all that changed. The possibilities were always there. When, where and how is not pertinent to an understanding of the mountain. There will always be a some kind of background noise we all have to try to hear through and over to the sound of the good chimes that ring in our own hearts. It just takes a little intention on our part to open to the possibility in the first place. Maybe all spiritual growth is about is finding the path to where the controls are and understanding that there exists a unique set for each of us to be used along our way through life; leading somehow to our ultimate goal, or what ever we individually conceive of as our next step to the next mountain in our never-ending path towards the light. I understand I'm not able to compel, wish, command or order the sun to shine today. I don't have a toggle switch that I can simply flip up or down or a set of knobs to dial in a perfect day. There's no remote control that can be tossed around my living room person to person so all in the room are able to tune to their idea of blissful comfort. There's a mountain top in Georgia you can go to and if it's a clear day, they say you can see three states. You can circumnavigate the globe, you can do it on a mountain bike, but that in itself holds no guarantee to finding a way to what I'm talking about. It might even drive you further away depending from where the energy source originates for such a task. That's not close to the process or even the goal. It sure took me a long time to learn that, but I did. I admit I hung around the doorsteps to the foundations, the icons to human enterprise and anybody or anything else with the ability to drown out the simple truths my own heart kept trying to convey to me, that all the answers I really need are just inside the doorway of my own heart. Finding out it's there and learning how to open it is the hard part. But hey, well, once you find it you see it everywhere. All you ever have to do is pull over to the side of the road and let it catch you. Just be still enough to, stay in one place long enough to feel your own pulse, to see something still and infinite wherever you are, something with that simple of a purpose can be your path to a kind of ecstasy.

There had been tons of healing moisture and coolness applied lovingly layer by layer to my mountain in the last couple of weeks. Isn't it just a miracle how all that happens? The sky just opens up and the rain starts to fall. It, maybe it's Nature talking here, says it has this thing it's going to need to do for a while. It doesn't ask permission or try to schedule an appointment. It doesn't take a survey or try to solicit volunteers. It's a natural process. It just rains. And as it rains it heals. It smooths out the rough spots, it mixes up the leaves from Fall, makes them soft to chew by the millions of unseen microscopic forest critters. The rain applies the needed weight to help the trees release some withered and unneeded branches; it cleans the streams. Like some magic medicinal water it soaks the acorn and calls forth the newborn taproot to drink its life from the moisture-laden soil and offers perfectly prepared formula of compost laid on by loving hands.

It must all be important, even the sound of steadily falling rain must vibrate some ancient communication to all the forest and all of those who live in that world feel the sound of the rains and are penetrated by their therapeutic power of rejuvenation. The forest becomes a kind of spa for all its inhabitants. The rains massage each molecule of forest matter, it moves all things into their proper alignment and connects like a billion threaded tapestry each filament of the forest into the majestic work of art it is. On this, its annual sabbatical to moisture it just sinks a little deeper into the earth, it becomes a little smaller and its connection to the earth itself a little stronger, surer, renewed to face the next season of never ending life.

The mountain is my brother, at least we have the same Father. A time will come one day when we, together, can share the oneness we both are destined to experience. But first there is a process in which we both will need to travel through. This process is called evaporation.

Chapter 19

Where Numbers Lose Their Meaning

🚲 🚲 🚲

I suppose I'd ridden right by it at least 500 times. It was at a place on the mountain bike trail that instead of the single-track, the path widens enough to accommodate automobile traffic down this really beautiful dirt road. On the park map of trails it's simply called Camp Road. But this place I'm about to describe to you, you'd never ever guess it was there. Funny, I had taken a picture of this place on the road because I'd noticed one day a small square piece of wood with the number five carved into it. That was more than a year ago. It was painted red on orange, just about five inches square, nailed, sim-

ply nailed about six or seven feet up from the ground to a tree. I took
a picture of it and called it "Where Numbers Lose Their Meaning." It
made no sense to me. I didn't know why it was there. The number
five all by itself, nailed to a tree on the side of a dirt road, right here
in the middle of nowhere. I thought my title appropriate, descriptive.

I come to the park to ride my mountain bike often. I'm not in to
going real fast. For me, its about time enjoyment and relaxation, its
about doing something that cures my mind, strengthens my soul and
at the same time helps to keep me in a program of exercise that I can
do to keep me healthy. Like I said, I'd seen that number five many
times, coming and going. Most of the time, because of where it is, it's
in a place where it's pretty flat for about a mile and a half where you
can really get some speed going on that small section of the mountain
bike trail. For me, that's about 12 miles an hour coasting by the number that has no meaning. Most of the time I never even notice it.
When I don't notice it, it's still there. It's there right now while I'm
writing this. It's alive somehow. It's being is alive right now in you as
you read theses words about it.

Then one morning I was on about my 500th time passing unmind-
fully this number hanging in the air. I don't know what made me slow
down. I don't known what made me stop right there. I wasn't thinking about it. I was on my way back to my starting point. I had about
two miles yet to go. It was just another perfect morning. Like so many
others, I was feeling good. Morning mountain bike rides are to me
one of the most refreshing experiences there are. The cool moistness,
the still clean air, the so satisfying sound of air passing all around you
like your standing in front of a huge fan. Coasting in another world
full of green and life. The rays of the morning sun streaking from the
forest floor right up to the tops of the trees where the rising mist
meets the cover that shades all who pass these ways. In other words,
what I'm struggling to say here, is that, just when I thought it couldn't
get any better, it did.

After I'd stopped completely, I got off my bike and while still holding on to it with one hand, found the nozzle of my hydration pack with

the other and began to take a long cool drink of water from its tube. While doing so and feeling the cold liquid pass through my throat down to my stomach, I leaned a little forward resting an elbow to my bike seat and stretched my back muscles at the same time. There I began a stretch that felt so good as my neck extended and my head twisted to the right and then slowly back to the left extending the muscles and feeling a bunch of good things all over as I extended my head down, bending further at the waist until my left hand found the ground and my right shoulder stretched across my chest releasing strain and some kind of endorphin mix right into my brain and throughout my whole body. I undid the chinstrap to my helmet, pulling it from my head and circled one end around a couple of times securing it to the handlebar while continuing to generally elongate my collection of muscles. It was about the third time I turned my head to the left that I saw it, an orange trail marker that I had never noticed before. Small trees and brush beside the road had grown up around it and about the only way anyone would ever notice it would to be in the position I found myself right then, twisting like a pretzel beside a mountain bike. Feeling the release in my back I straighten myself and stepped a little closer to what I was making out to be a path, a path I'd never noticed, not in 500 times going right by it. As I moved to its opening I let my bike ease to the ground, sliding it behind me, dragging it like the toy it was, just a couple of feet off the road along side the small red oak tree where a heavy slap of orange paint hid beneath its overgrown branches. I could barely see into it, but there was a path here. It was a horse trail. That's what the color orange means out here. The thing is that most people who ride horses here rarely venture this far from the stable and the trails near there. I'd happened upon an almost totally unused trail, not a hoof-print in sight, but it was here. It was maintained just enough not to disappear. "Just like me," I would think later. The small narrow path, here at the opening, was barely large enough for me to pass, much less a horse and a rider, I thought as I moved downward to about four feet below the level of the road, following this path's snakelike direction. Just ten feet in and looking back I could barely see my bike, so thick the growth of branches and with a couple of well placed bushes, made it, a few more feet in, almost impossible to see the road I'd just come down from.

It was dark here. It was cool. There was a large birch tree just across the other side of an S-shaped section of stream that was crackling over shallow rocks right at my feet. I noticed thick tree roots that looked like the tentacles of an octopus burying itself just below the shallow level of the water until they disappeared underground. With a fair amount of caution I walked very slowly towards the shoreline of the creek. I watched carefully my own footsteps venturing forward, mindful of the possibility of perhaps disturbing natural inhabitants of this scene. I inched my way to the shoreline of the creek and gauged the water surface to be about eight feet across. Right there, greeting me was a shallow, slowly moving wide section of still-like water reflecting glimmers of refracted light that snuck through the low cover of branches from towering trees. The sound of water bubbling over shallow rocks was coming up from my left and down to my right where this stream meandered gently downward, away and quickly out of my view. I felt like I had discovered something. Something very few people had ever seen just beyond the place I had called "Where Numbers Lose Their Meaning."

As I stood there in this place all the fatigue from my bike riding had melted away. There was a coolness I was being absorbed into. The quiet sounds of the water were vibrating some kind of verbal message that seemed to pierce me and cleanse me at the same time. I looked across the creek, saw through the still water there down to the creek bed that was covered with flat stones all the way across to the rising ground on the other side. The trail moved up past and around the large many rooted birch, behind it and disappeared along a hillside twenty feet from the opposite shore.

I was in a special room, closed off to the rest of the path, the rest of the park and completely from the rest of the world. "Wow!" I said out loud and at the same time twisted as to turn back to the road and followed with, "this is the most beautiful place in the world." Right then I began to laugh. I really laughed and then for some unknown reason I felt myself, I felt it in my chest and then all over something indescribable that made me stop laughing and I began to cry, to weep like I don't know what. It wasn't like I was sad; it was just that I was overpowered by something so beautiful that crying was my only response. It was wonderful. It was like I had been given some incredible gift and I just wasn't expecting it, I didn't know how to react. I was suddenly just plain overwhelmed by all this surrounding beauty. I enjoyed it and I was thankful I was able to feel all this around me so completely.

I felt like I'd happened upon some mythological, magical place that has always existed throughout the wide expanses of time and space. I was in the Garden of Eden. I was where unicorns stopped to drink. I felt the eyes of gods. I was seeing into a portal to true peace and love. I felt a physical, a real, a tangible connection from the middle of my chest to the infinite. I was standing right in the middle of a miracle. I was standing in some spiritual vortex created just for me, just for me right now to use like an ageless communication device connected directly to the center of universal intelligence. To-you-know-what-I-mean! I was separating from one reality to another. I was spinning away from it right then and there. I was falling away from the confines of my preconceptions to endless possibilities, uncountable opportunities, and total forgiveness. All the problems of my life, I felt myself releasing them to this force as I fell to my knees feeling like I was truly loved for the first time in my life. Numbers had no meaning here. They had no meaning at all.

I was down a different path than the one a few yards away where I'd laid down my bike just a couple of minutes earlier. So different it was. So peacefully quiet. I let myself become the place. I breathed it in. I let my self find its seat and relax there by this gentle slowly moving water. I made myself; I seemed to feel myself fusing with this place, with these sounds and sights. I was in a timeless place where, as I fell deeper into its trance, I was becoming, I seemed to feel myself flowing into these surroundings. I was becoming lighter and lighter, cleaner and clearer as sporadic rays of sunlight penciled the water surface before me. I saw diamond-like reflections of white light dance around me like some percolating energy being released from some cosmic engine that was used to drive the universe. It was just under the surface. It had always existed here. I watched it rise and fall. I felt the understated power of it. I knew it was boundless and I felt connected to it. The connection was strong here as I moved faster within this magic stillness. And there I sat, going deeper into contentment, melting into my surroundings, feeling my mind become like some finely tuned instrument in harmony with a complete symphony of masterfully orchestrated enchantment. I was at its center from where I could see into eternity and all it took was to simply be in stillness with this place along my pathway. All it took was a moment to stop and let the universe catch up with me, to let myself hear its call, to let the peaceful side of my nature rule for just long enough to quiet the needs of everyday stress, turmoil and fear. That's what happened. I let all that go. It drifted away from me like a cloud of mist on to the ground before me. It just melted away into the water of the stream and then was taken up by the roots of many trees and floated out through its branches and leaves as high above sunlight evaporated it all into clean clear air. I watched it all and sighed.

Moments later I was back on the bike path moving a little faster and feeling so much lighter. A little while from now I'd be on another path. I felt my excitement growing for whatever the new day held before me. I was prepared for whatever it might bring. The world was a beautiful place. Already this day I had discovered a place I'd overlooked many times before. I knew there must be other places where other numbers could lose their own meanings in time. The possibilities were infinite. They always had been.

Chapter 20

Traveling Light

I was starting to get that warmed up feeling. It usually takes about a half an hour of exercise before everything about me begins to feel right for the ride ahead. It's at that time where the pace of my breathing has been established for the day's ride and my air exchange apparatus becomes akin to an old fashioned pair of bellows you might use to keep a fire at a constant temperature; the in and out stream of air that provides oxygen to blood and further along to the muscles that drives me forward. By that time all my muscles and bones have climbed aboard and have found agreement with my brain. All of me wants to do what I'm doing right now. My mountain bike is adequate to its task. I should have adjusted my brakes before I started out but I should have done that really about ten or fifteen rides ago. It didn't matter, they would be okay for today. This was just going to be a ten- or twelve-miler in the early morning light and the brand new air, a Monday morning, the last week in June. "God I love this."

It had been a few years since my first experience with mountain biking. In the beginning it was, for me, about trying to get into shape more than anything. I looked at my watch a lot in those days. I was confused. I thought mountain biking was mostly about how far-how fast concepts. I believed it was mostly about physical exercise, a way to stay in shape mostly, fun, but it had this business side that it took a while for me to put into perspective. I hadn't thought about what else this activity would end up doing for me. I measured my pulse and heart rate a lot. My wristwatch came in handy. Today I don't even wear one.

One day I was out riding when I got a little too close to a tree while in a left turn. It wasn't the first time. As it happened, like it happened a few times previously, my left forearm, including my wrist, brushed up against a tree and that little hit, on top of many others became the last straw for the integrity of my stainless steel bracelet. I stopped and picked it up of course. I remember standing there, finding it easily in the pine straw, picking it up and observing where the steel pin that had held the bracelet to the watchcase had broken away, the metal was twisted, my arm was okay. For a moment there I held it in my hand, feeling its metallic weight pressing into my hand. Unconsciously I was weighing it. Then quite consciously I bounced it in my open hand, listened to the steel-on-steel sound it made, closed my gloved fist around it and opened my hand to see its shiny face. It was then I realized it. Right then, right there, I didn't care what this watch had to say anymore, to me, or to anybody else. There were plenty of places where I could find out what time it was, clocks after all, are everywhere. Just then the one inside of me said I wanted to get moving so I put the old watch with the broken bracelet in the zippered accessory bag underneath my bike seat and rolled back on to my bike and away. The whole deal took less than a minute. At least that's what I'm guessing; the time had come when I no longer wore a watch.

Moving back down the trail I began to feel a kind of lightness, a new flavor of freedom as I thought about how long it took me to get to that point back there where I crashed my watch. I thought about why I ever started wearing a watch in the first place. Are we born asking what time it is? Yes, probably, but we do so many things in our life without thinking why. The herding instinct is strong. Lately, these days, I had been reviewing what seemed to most people much larger decisions about where I wanted the rest of my life to go. My biking experiences, in their own little way had helped me to discover more than the many great things to see and feel out here in the woods, but had also provided a kind of sanctuary to meditate about what was really important and what I wanted to do about it. Riding this mountain bike was a front row seat to a place where I could think to myself and let my ideas, whatever they might consist of at the time, bloom into life. I found out here ideas were the same as dreams and that the way to make your dreams come true was to simply act upon them. Create a plan and follow through. And that was what I had been doing. And for the last ten months, that was what I had been doing full time. This path I'm riding right now ride is a dream come true. The Bike Path itself is a dream and then some!

Some days it's oh-so-clear. If you were to look down from the air, just above the treetops, it is all but impossible to see a lone mountain biker sailing along these paths. The overgrowth, the green canopy of full summer easily conceals a lone rider below. Yet in my vision of all this I'm able to, in my imagination, see right through the heavy growth of tree limbs and their immense growth of leaves. In my mind I can see right through those things like unraveling layers of gauze. I unwind them to see him moving effortless along the single-track. From high above the tops of these trees he looks so small as he skill-fully leans in and down through a left turning switchback, gliding with speed up high into the turn and shooting downward and back to the right, maneuvering effortlessly along a meandering downhill run towards what's left of ruins of what was a cabin in these woods a hundred years ago; right past its stone fireplace, its chimney, now overgrown right up to the edge of his passage. There he goes. I see him clearly picking up speed, rising up from his seat, his knees bent and his body weight shifting backwards towards his rear tire. I see his front end, the tire bounce up and down with almost all of the movement being absorbed by the large front-end shock absorber. The shock is working overtime absorbing the waves of tree roots that cover this part of a mildly descending single-track. While that is going on the rider is loosely holding on to the steady handlebars, applying the brakes and shifting gears, maintaining all the time a velocity perfectly in tune to the trail conditions presented on this perfect day. I see him speeding up and slowing down constantly changing, moving over the bikes frame locking up the rear wheel and sliding a fish tail around a corner. I can count the individual, stopped in action spokes and see the gravel fly, the dust rise and the punctuating tire mark being drawn in the trail, brushed in as if it was applied by an artist's hand. In a way, our rider is the artist himself, he is the creator of this time, these moments where his creative vision is met and put upon not only this magnificent canvas, the bike path, but somehow finds its way to me and to you. We watch with true excitement and anticipation as he simply speeds along.

There is a rhythm to all this that you can hear. When it's all in tune, the trail, the bike and the rider, you sense most powerfully the sounds of rushing air all around you. To me, it's like standing in the bow of a sailboat. A mountain bike is a kind of a sailboat, I think to myself, as I see our rider below tacking his way upward along the mountain trail. I can hear his rate of breathing increase as he digs down deeper for a controlled rhythmic pace that will take him to the top of this hill. From my vantage point, as I swing around above him, I can see an expression of relaxed determination on his face, I can hear the smooth sound of metal working underneath with metal, I can feel the tension of it stretching to its capabilities, working here perfectly as envisioned. There's the sweat. What a climber!

All around there is the forest, in its fullest splendor laid out below me like a lumpy blanket tossed away carelessly by a child. It's a solid green today. I do so admire it as I fly high above, see it all, take it all in as I rise even higher until I almost lose it from my sight, clearly seeing, from my vantage point, that this mountain of mine is just a small part of even larger mountain ranges amongst further stretching patchquilts of farms and forest. But like a magnet, no matter how far or how high I go, the mountain draws me to it, back to its magic spirit filled world.

Falling downward through the trees I easily find our rider. Now, this time, I can feel the heat of August rising up to me, and being almost overcome as I watch him burst on to the fire road at the top of my mountain. Today he's turning right and beginning to come up to speed as I hear the sounds of gears changing, the fluttering of his bike chain being lifted to a higher gear. It's around noontime and the dust is rising behind our rider, being picked up and formed into a smoky tail as he cuts his way through the thin sharp air. It is so completely dry. The creeks than ran overflowing their beds a couple of months ago are, in places, completely void of moisture and in other places single shallow pools of still water seem to be in wait of the inevitability that encircles. This is the time of the year when some varieties of pine trees loose their needles; they shower them down upon the dirt roads and trails painting them a rusty red. The heat from these patches combines with a special seasonal song as fast bike tires harmonize with the crushing sound of compressed dryness. A spicy fragrance rises to your face. You can taste it on your tongue.

Through this mirage of searing heat, this wavy unfocused confused distortion of vision, I see him churning along the dirt road at the top of his mountain, moving through a sea of shorter, shade less alpine like vegetation, slash and short needled pines oven baked in the full of the noonday sun. I see him moving, tires sinking into deeper sand turned white by the ageless sun, but moving without pause, complete with an unspoken but determined mindful purpose. There, as he moves, I see him drinking deeply from the tube of his hydration backpack. I see him use its hose to apply to himself, all across the front of his chest and down his back, a hard spray of the cool water, and as he does he keeps his steady pace, continually moving forward, legs ever churning.

Before us, about a half a mile away, we see high above, the sight of two slowly circling black winged buzzards. Effortlessly they ride the rising heat thermals of midday, dipping their wings as they float in some kind of station keeping dance above, leaning in and leaning over. Just a bit early for their appointment, they float on patience itself; all knowing, seasoned in their approach to this day's welcomed meal. Their mere presence with us becomes a simple statement about life above and death below. We wonder at nature's profound consistency and our understanding, our connection within the plan of plans. All existence is so fragile. Which of us are more like the gods we wonder? They fly. We ride.

We continue to ride through the summer to fall, just before Thanksgiving and from my viewpoint the mountain has transformed. I see the vivid reds, yellow and orange splashed about masterfully upon the canvas canopy that shades still all that move and breath underneath its shelter. Moving through this whirlpool of colors to the trails below I feel the seasonal wind, the new coolness it carries and I hear it constantly above me in the treetops. It sways the drying branches, losing the leaves' grip to life in preparation for the coming of winter. But today he's out there. He's in here flying down the fire road headed to turn right on to the black diamond downhill single-track, the most dangerous part of the course.

Blood Rock is calling him again, daring him to try. Taunting him with its legends of human failure. It's degree of danger unmatched and uncontested, especially by those who have tried and failed, who've left their own blood trails and added entry to the long list of broken collar bones and worse. But here he goes, flying off the road and into the air dropping like a bird of prey on to the thin line of the path that leads down to his challenge. Everything compresses and the force of his landing is perfectly absorbed by heavy-duty shock

absorbers and by the well-conditioned muscles and tendons of a finely
tuned athlete. His mind is so right today. He's headed down the
mountain alone. He's headed where few dare to even ride. He is going
as fast as he can go, through the two tight turns left and right and
ever down the steepest slope around where both small and huge rocks
have percolated out from an ageless trail on an ageless mountain;
where a creek runs quickly over shiny rocks producing even more
hazard and fear. In fact, fear is everywhere. At Blood Rock it has a
physical body. It moves all over you. It crawls upon your soul and
stares you in the eye defiant, hungry for another victim it welcomes
you down to where there is no turning back, no stopping to reconsid-
er, because at the speed you're going now stopping here, on this rocky
grade over slippery wet rocks is impossible. But that's exactly why
he's here and for our rider being, doing this is a statement about what
he's about as a human being, a mountain biker.

Watching him move down there is simple, quiet, undeniable evidence of our collective innate need to challenge ourselves. We need it
to exist. The need is part of us like eye color and ear shape, that make
up our physical appearance, the desire to excel in a thing that, whatever it is, is part of who we are. Risk just comes with the territory and
much is being risked right now as our rider's plan to live through the
experience actuates itself to motion. He's not thinking too much about
the danger. He's not hearing the mountain's taunts. The images in his
mind right now don't include the crash victims remains splayed out by
the rocky blade that is the unmistakable namesake of this place, this
arena where no one observes but us. He's not here for us. He's here
for only himself and it shows so well. All these things gel into a fluid
motion of a cross between a ballet dancer and a middle linebacker. All
the strength of both combine with instantaneous judgment, inexhaustible courage, fluid coordination and boundless enthusiasm. If
you could see it in slow motion you could see him applying both front
and rear brakes instantaneously, together, separately and not at all,
flying in the air over much of the danger, picking his launch and his
landings instantly together, combining in the only possible combina-

tion to maneuver these deadly hazards without harm. He makes it look so easy. Headed down and away from us he clears the last rocky drop down to the sanctuary and security of solid ground, then a hard hard left and still headed down slope speeds off on to the old quarry road with more bumps and jumps just ahead.

What a world and time to ride. The colors here are indescribable today. Cut out from the cliff, the quarry road, with the exception of a couple of easy turns, is mostly a straight line down. Off to the left huge lichen covered limestone boulders punctuate the dark shade cliffs that beckon you upward to the mountain summits. To the right you can look straight down the mountainside itself, nervously feel the steepness of it at its edge. You can see the tops of colorful trees falling off and away, filling this huge fruit bowl of the valley below. The pine trees that were much a part of the scenery on the mountaintop above, have all but been replaced by these oaks, poplars, white barked birches and other hardwood species. Throughout, looking both up and down both sides of the road, groups of large leafed spreading green ferns vibrate along waves from a gentle breeze, here, there, everywhere they spot the shady hillside forest floor looking akin to shimmering schools of tropical fish. We're simply in awe of all that surrounds us here and almost forget to watch our biker hop one more time high in the air, celebrating in action his victory over this mountain. We see him take to the airways bouncing up and over man made berms, back down to hidden single-track, then lastly, as he moves away, we hear the now dimming hum of swiftly turning mountain bike tires slanting down and into the forest deep and lost. Woosh...winter's on its way.

Early this morning, it presents itself in stillness. The once-emerald green forest has weathered into a purified grey. It blurs all the lines between matter and air. The now lost colors of a fall have faded to grey-blacks and browns. Passing by the lake we see wisps of frozen air kick around its solidified surface, veins of white track across its cover from the shoreline out to a silver forbidding center. Above, the morning sky is equally intimidating, low lying clouds move with speed, chilling all who brave to look upon its power. The Earth is being sterilized today.

Somewhere, from deep inside the season there is heard an ancient calling, soundless it speaks volumes to the soul. It's an open invitation to pick up the trail again, to make that inner journey to the place that leads to the promised land.

Our rider hears the call once more and sets off to stitch another thread to his commitment, to become again the solitary explorer and renew his inner being. Paradise, he knows, is not a myth, it's just a shift in mind. As he passes the lake and enters the woods we see he's dressed appropriately for the day and it doesn't take him long to energize and warm himself as he marches his movements up to speed.

The woods are really frozen hard this day. Just the light wind above is enough to provide a background of cracking noise from the trees that combines with the crunchy sound of frozen tires pressing into the percolated icy moisture; bleeding today, so profusely up from the frosty ground. There won't be other riders out here today. Most people are intimidated, weather-wise, by any climate or temperatures that can't be controlled by just twisting the dial of a hallway thermostat. Weather is the first line of defense as reasons why so many positive things never happen or become obtainable. Too hot, too cold, too wet, too dry or not enough of any, either or all. Our rider knows well that trap into blank existence, blind acceptance. He has chosen to listen elsewhere for a calling that originates from higher ground. He sees things today that most people never will, he sees the heart of nature ever beating despite this shroud of cold. He observes the scattered fur of what yesterday held a life. He's out here today to be observant of it all. On and on he spins it until he reaches the frozen center to the world. This is what he came for to be right here in this place, to connect and refocus on what's important, what's real and reaffirm where all that is.

The bridge here over this creek is a place he discovered some years ago. On sunny mornings he would come here, like today, for peace and real quiet, watch the running water below and wave back and forth to his shadow. You know the place I mean. This morning, deep in winter, the creek was thinly frozen over, he can see water flowing beneath the ice. He picks out moving air bubbles just beneath its surface. They look like amoebas under a microscope, they look alive being propelled by the pressure of the flowing water. There's no reflection from the surface today, the conditions being what they are, but his search doesn't stop there, here, in his special peaceful place, there's so much room to see inside.

From my vantage point, I couldn't tell exactly what went on down there for a while. But through the heavy fog I could make out some things. Down there I watched him seem to relax and lean on to the edge of the bridge resting his upper body weight on his elbows, his head bowed. After a minute or two, it looked like he placed his face into his open hands. I could see him lightly shake. He stayed that way for a couple of minutes more at least. I'm not sure, but to me, it looked like he was crying. I don't know. It was just a very few minutes altogether that he paused there and after those minutes he walked away very slowly, pausing once to look back to the empty bridge almost as if he never wanted to leave or added something that he'd forgot to say. I don't know, it was pretty foggy down there, but he soon got back on his bike and returned up the trail the same way he came.

He was really moving this time. There seemed to be a new fluidness about his movement. Maybe it was so evident contrasted against all the backdrop of these special woods at ten degrees. Maybe something heavy fell off of him back there at that bridge. No doubt though to this observer he was back in the world. Just watching him move along was really heightening my own sense about how a little extra speed can change a ride in the park into the ride of your life. There was no carelessness here, don't get me wrong. What I was watching was a moving picture of controlled calculated explosions of joy. Seeing him moving this way, clad head to toe in all this winter wear, dressed in black, only his eyes exposed to the freezing cold, it was easy for me to imagine he and the bike as one. It all was moving so smoothly now along the forest path. It was as if the universal powers had ordained, had called for some sort of hybrid mechanism to exploit some yet undiscovered connecting point where man, nature and machines might merge. Maybe oneness is what happens, what it looks like in our worldly eyes, when we able or granted by high permission, to see a spirit fly.

Personally, I love winter. I think it's my favorite time of the year to be outdoors. There is something in me that drives me to the woods and on my own bike in the wintertime. One of my favorite things about winter is how wonderful Spring feels right up next to it. One day you're out there in all that long sleeved layered look and the next day you're feeling the hint of warm air in the late afternoon. The smiling yellow-faced daffodils tell the whole story; the cold air of late February is transfused with the life-force from a budding leaf. The woods take on a furry yellow light green and in some places I feel like I'm riding right in the middle of a perfume factory. By the beginning of April all is transformed and ready for that official first rider of Spring.

From way up here I can look down on my favorite mountain just as the morning mist and the temperature starts to rise. I see through a yellow pollen-filled sky down once more to that magical place along the mountain top and from there it's an easy slide through the thickening layers of newborn leaves, through oxygen's rich beginnings, the gleaming first slice of the morning sunlight, illuminating all in this most perfect living world. Just as I ease myself in to my front row seat, I pick him out moving swiftly into an easy turn.

The spring showers have been kind to the woods and the streams are full to overflowing, everywhere their vibrations are clean, producing freshness and loving familiarity, an annual transfusion of nurturing to all and all parts of these surroundings, to living beings, who for their very existence, on these running waters, they depend. In spring it's easy to see the interconnectedness of these things. On a moving mountain bike you see it all moving before you like some movie that you're the star in. The narrow single-track you ride looks like a shiny green tunnel sometimes and you can feel the plant-life reaching out and touching you, in some places pushing you along, you're in the narrow part of nature's horn of plenty, it's like being rocked in a mothers arms.

Then, it can be so sudden. You see the first of the first deer you'll see today. She's startled and takes off running. She's not thinking of where she's going, just away from you. Just over the next hill disappearing thinking she has seen the last of you, but you turn another corner and she's standing there quite frozen, in the middle of the trail, neither of you knowing what to do. I can see our rider slow it down, ease it quietly and stop. Twenty feet in front of him there is a hundred and fifty-something-pound doe, with the biggest brown eyes you weren't ever expecting to see looking straight at you unable to even move. That's what they do, what they're famous for, they freeze.

Our rider's movement shifts way down to slow motion and in the softest voice, like a whisper within a smile, he breathes "good morning." From where you are you think that maybe, they've met before. As soon as you make that observation you notice that there are other deer around. Up to the right, one, two, there's a third one, he's a spike, the small horns obvious even from where you are. Then you catch a movement just below you, four, five, six, another almost movement, a pair of white spotted fawns ambling around on shaky legs...you're surrounded, in the middle of somebody else's den. You smile a little wider, nodding inwardly with the realization, that you were absolutely mistaken in thinking that you were riding here alone. Not alone at all, quite conversely, you've been running with the herd.

This is one of those really cool unexpected encounters that you'll never get tired of or jaded by. Each time it happens it's special, it's a magic bubble and you're inside. One moment you're riding alone and suddenly there is a full-grown buck running as fast as it can right beside you, along with you in the same direction, his antlers beside your handlebars moving together down a single-track. You hear its heavy breathing, smell its musky odor, you hear its hooves tearing up the dirt and then as quick as it appeared, it jumps right in front of you and in a couple of leaping bounds, it's over the top the hillside and gone. And so are you, you're on another planet, a world within a world.

With just a little imagination out on the bike path it's pretty easy to think of each one of the four seasons as separate environments, distinct planets in separate solar systems. This green one full of pollen and perfume, inhabitants like deer, wild flying turkeys and the rest of all the out and about wildlife, it's all just so available and visible this time of year. Spring is an ever-unfolding play about renewal and new discoveries. This planet named Spring, with its soul habitant moving confidently about one of its most beautiful mountains, in, around, through the peaceful valley up the draws where last night's wind focused its strength laying down at last a lichen covered limbless oak to be found here as just transformed punctuation for the path; brilliantly he takes to the air and pitches his front tire spinning right sideways in salute to this finally fallen mass.

Today, the main course on this riders menu will be a the downhill. How humorous a description. Headed downhill in most conversations usually refers to something less than desirable. But here, not the case at all, in fact, this may be the centerpiece of this whole activity, mountain biking. In just over two miles he's going to drop about two thousand feet. This is dangerous stuff with speed. This is dangerous enough without it. Have a flat tire, fishtail on some loose rocks, sink in heavy deep sand just enough to turn a front tire when you don't want to and you have a whole bunch of new problems. Twenty miles per hour on a mountain bike going downhill is a thrill you will forever remember if you live to tell about it. If you don't know it already you need to know that when you're going that fast straight down a hill over loose gravel, at that point when you hit the rut in the road and your handlebars start to vibrate and shake like they're coming apart, when you feel the rear end of your bike dancing the jitterbug above all the washed out gravel, when, in all this mess of saturated brake pads from powering into and out of streambeds, it occurs to you that your brakes no longer work as designed, it's way to late do anything but hold on as best as you can. Translate "as best as you can" into "for dear life". But think about it, right there in the middle of that road, for at least a few terrifying moments, you now and forever will know completely and intimately just what it fells like to be a bullet. That's kind of special.

Our rider has already traveled fifteen miles this morning. He's seen things today that most people never will and that's what he is thinking and being so profoundly thankful for as he sits atop his bike, balanced even in stillness here, a foot resting on a rock, taking a well deserved drink, calming down and reaching his quiet center just before he pushes off to down. I can see his shoulders rise and fall, the marking of his preparing centering breaths. He just looks like completely ready as he seems to let himself relax into gravity like a little ball that's about to roll down a gentle hill. Slowly, cautiously always, he lets the downward slope of the mountain road move him into speed.

Somewhere in the expanse of space an asteroid tumbles past a comet's tail on its way to nowhere fast. The last ray of light from the remnant of an exploded sun falls silently on that tumbling world. The pressure of that ray of light against the frozen metal rock redefines the characteristics of its invisible pressure wave through space. This theoretical ripple, a trillion light years away, stimulates an electron stream that speeds off and to our time as it intersects with earth. Our biker's path runs along a mountain stream that moves underneath a bridge. He's outrunning the rushing water, he's faster than the wind. He's guided by unseen forces that he feels inside his heart. He knows his soul and its connection to the entire universe here and beyond the trail. And here, right here is where he can feel it most intensely, where it permeates his body, where it blends with his inner being and makes him more than just mortal. He becomes another being, he's becomes connected with all there is out there, he's colliding and exploding rising high into the air. He's a example of a promise fulfilled that's made to one's own self, he's a picture of a perfected multitude of connected moments strung together here in a line moving swiftly down a mountain. What a thing to see.

From our vantage point, just above the tree tops, we can see him begin his charge down the mountain. Faster and faster he moves along the downhill run. We see an almost continuous trail of dust rising behind him looking almost like the exhaust of a jet engine curving through in flight just above the ground. We watch him as he expertly applies brakes and moves his body over his bike frame setting up each turn early and leaning in then out of the curve, playing the hop of his rear tire with style and finesse. Beside him the waters are rushing too. Down this mountain the road crosses seven streams that today will be swollen almost to their capacity. Seven times we'll get to watch him fly over every one of the wide crossings at full speed. That's the way he does it, approaches, compresses and flies completely over the rushing water and beyond, coming to earth well past the edge of the opposite shore. Then, just ahead, there is his favorite crossing where the road dips just before the creek so the approach to this one becomes in an instant an uphill run at his fastest speed. This is exactly what it looks like to be shot, blasted out of a cannon at the circus. It's an explosion into flight, but unlike the circus, there's no net to fall into, only ground that is falling away further down the trail, a ski jump without the skis or snow. What a kick to tear the edges off all these envelopes of every day. What a thrill, what a privilege we think as we watch him fly through space as we learn to breathe again.

On this spring day he's just moving forward. Maybe that's what this is all about as we see him slowing down, as if to make it last. In a few hundred yards it will be all over. The end's the big reminder to him that there are some things that never end and so are never really over. That's the big deal that he finally learned out here. He found it one day in a reflection down on the water in place inside his heart. He found it in the promise of these always changing living seasons and this beauty of every precious day. It was something that would forever gleam and he could carry to make him lighter through every season no matter what path he might take. The bike path is only one path that he travels on his journey to a wider world. Connected to himself and learning to be in every moment caries forward into his life and relationships with all he meets and loves. All those things are other stories that he considers deeply as he rides. He knows what's important. He's learned to feel with his heart and soul. The majority of his life is lived beyond the bike path but the balance that he's found here is available to him every where he goes.

Going away is where I guess it's appropriate to leave him. We've followed this guy, our rider, enough today. My ride too today is finished. For me, myself and I, we've all got a lot to do. Today we've watched the seasons change through other peoples eyes and our own. We've been up on the mountain and down and it's only eight a.m. The rest of the day is waiting with its lists of things to do. I'll start by putting this broken watch in the kitchen junk drawer and asking God where to go from there.

The Bike Path

By Wayne Eliot Lankford

It seemed like such a simple thing
When I learned how to ride a bike
But it ended up on a mountain top
Where I'd just never seen the like

It was truly the road less traveled
In fact it was just a path
But when it took me and what I felt
There weren't any questions asked

I was in the lead up here
Wasn't just following along
This thing had grabbed me by the heart
My wheels supplied the song

Yea, I've been up on the mountain
And I saw the truth revealed
The Bike Path told me many things
Like how to truly feel

As I ride the trails today
And I truly touch this space
I'm on the mountain once again
The Bike Path is my place

I can connect so well to the spirits here
And thus to so much more
The feelings were always inside of me
The Bike Path is the door

Epilogue

The epilogue is suppose to be the place, usually at the end of a play or like here at the end of a book, where the author or some of the actors come out on to the stage and meet with their audience for a little while; maybe answer some questions or let them in on some information about how the play came about in the first place. I believe most all that information was supplied in the first part of this book. What I wanted to do here is just briefly tell you where in the physical world the bike path I call home is located and a little bit about it.

The parking lot where I park my car and un-rack my mountain bike is in a beautiful place called Oak Mountain State Park in Pelham Alabama, just south of Birmingham. It is comprised of nearly ten thousand acres of heavily wooded forest land. There are lakes there, camping facilities, cabins, boating and fishing activities, hiking trails, a BMX track, road biking paths alongside all the paved roads inside the park, picnicking areas and a world renowned Wildlife Center. The Wildlife Center at OMSP helps over 2,500 animals a year. Anne Miller, its Executive Director, has spent twenty-five years caring for animals. One day they'll erect a statue of Anne for her pioneering efforts towards the caring and nurturing of injured and orphaned animals. Then of course, there is the seventeen miles of the most beautiful and well maintained mountain bike trail in the world. Keener Morrow, OMSP Naturalist, understands the ecological inter-connectedness of all elements, human and non-human, that must be respected for the park to stay healthy. Like Anne, he's out there every day committed to seeing that all us will be able to enjoy this wonderful place for a very long time.

For only two dollars you can spend the day at Oak Mountain. A few dollars more will get you a campsite, a little more a cabin. There are many new hotels and a variety of restaurants within a mile or two of the trailheads. There is no information available as to the number of mountain bikers who ride the OMSP trails every year. All I can tell you is that I have never been out there when I've felt like it was crowded at all. Conversely, if you were to ride there any weekday morning (M - F) you or your group might do the whole loop without seeing another human being.

I have met people from all over the United States out on the bike trails at Oak Mountain. I have been told that it is rated consistently as one of the top ten single-track trails in the USA. Over the last few years I have ridden out there on the average at least 3 times a week, for me that's close to ten thousand miles out there on that mountain. It is different every time I ride it. Regardless of the season, the mountain maintains its ageless beauty.

The trails are almost completely maintained by volunteers consisting primarily of members of The Birmingham Urban Mountain Peddlers or B.U.M.P. This group is also responsible for much of the aesthetics of the trail that so many people enjoy. Without BUMP there probably would not be a bike path at OMSP, that's how important BUMP and other volunteers are to maintaining mountain bike trails, not just at Oak Mountain, but everywhere. Once a year, usually in the first part of June, they organize and put on what has become one of the premier mountain biking races in the United States, the Bump N' Grind. Here professional and amateur riders converge for a weekend to celebrate this activity. Every year it gets bigger and better.

That's about all I wanted to say in this epilogue. I've got to go ride my bike. But before I go I wanted to let you know that I understand that mountain biking is not for everybody. There are a bunch of physical activities people can do to keep themselves healthy; mountain biking is just one. My deal with this book is to celebrate the activity I discovered at a time in my life when I really needed an inspiration to keep going and be me for the first time in my life. Mountain biking provided that for me. I hope you'll try it, be so inspired by my descriptions of it that you'll maybe even let me know about it. More importantly, if you never ever even get on any kind of bicycle for the rest of your life but were somehow touched by what I've written here, I hope you'll let me know about that too. After all, we're all on paths to the same place.

Web Resources

The following web sites are listed here because I have found them to be informative and useful. Some of them are just plain fun. They are presented here in no particular order: (except for the first one)

The Bike Path - www.thebikepath.com
My own personal web site. Here you will be able to see more and in color.

Dirt Rag Magazine - www.dirtragmag.com
The alternative Mountain Biking Forum

Birmingham Urban Mountain Peddlers (B.U.M.P.)
www.bump.org/ My bike club.

Single Speed Outlaw - www.singlespeedoutlaw.com
Where one sprocket rules all.

Oak Mountain State Park - www.bham.net/oakmtn/
Informational website with all the hoop-la about my favorite place to ride.

Hooked On the Outdoors Magazine - www.ruhooked.com/
Lot's of good stuff!

International Mountain Biking Association - www.imba.com/
The name says it all.

Discover Mountain Biking Com -
www.discovermountainbiking.com/
Great website!

Mountain Biking Online - www.mountainbikingonline.com
Can you imagine what they celebrate on this website?

Bikes Belong - http://bikesbelong.org/
Groups like this one make sure that there will always someone speaking for our bikes.

The Chopra Center - http://www.chopra.com
I am a big fan of Dr. Deepak Chopra. He's about peace, love and happiness.

Pink Bike - www.pinkbike.com
One of the best places I know to surf to.

Joe Kurmaskie is the Metal Cowboy - www.metalcowboy.com/

MTBtour.org - http://mtbtour.org/
For the love of it!

www.zukav.com/
Gary Zukav has changed a lot of people's lives.

Pensacola Off-Road Cyclists - www.porc.org/
Great bunch of mountain bikers!

The Lance Armstrong Foundation fights cancer. www.laf.org

Southern Off Road Biking Association - www.sorba.org/home.asp

Coming Attractions from Oak Valley Press

Presently a coffee table stylebook edition of *The Bike Path* is being put together by Bruce Hyer for release in summer of 2004. By incorporating over 150 full color digital impressionistic photographs into the story line we believe we can produce a piece of art many people will want to add to their collection. The release date will be timed so as to insure its availability at retail for the 2004 Christmas season. We think of it as a great gift idea for people who love biking.

Because *The Bike Path* itself is a never-ending journey, its first sequel is planned to be released in 2005. *Further Along the Bike Path* will explore more deeply into the metaphysical aspects introduced in the first book.

A novel that explores some pretty serious subject matter is scheduled for completion and general release by the end of the first quarter of 2004. *Crane Hill* will take our rider off the bike path and into some unavoidable experiences, real and imagined. Mountain biking is simply the backdrop for this book about the sometimes mentally unacceptable circumstances that in some form, some time or another, will cross inevitably all of our paths. The first chapter is submitted here for your review.

To keep up to date with the author and upcoming events visit **www.thebikepath.com** for the latest information.

Take a look at the following sample from *Crane Hill*.

Crane Hill, a novel

By Wayne Eliot Lankford

Chapter 1

The News

It would prove to be like a jumping off a cliff, no, not jumping, like being thrown off screaming—that would better describe it.

Tuesday morning three weeks ago, the day started just fine, sailing down the trails early in the morning the last week in September, not a hint that I would soon find out about something so terrible. The leaves on some of the trees were turning, a couple of smaller varieties had already yellowed, highlighting the dark green of most of the thick foliage all around me as I trekked along my early morning ride. The trees were still wet from the previous night's rainstorm. The last gasps of its wind curled above me in the treetops and I was rewarded with cool drops of water that had clung to the leaves so high above, purposely there, until now, just to refresh me alone as I tacked up and away along these familiar hills that made up this rich and magical world. On top of the mountain the first rays of the morning sun were brilliant! The sharp rays of the new white light emphasized the rising fog of the warming earth and the sight of so many separate and sharp-

ened streaks coming down from the tops of the high trees just stopped
me dead in my track, there, just fixed me in wonder of all this ordi-
nary everyday magic. Wow! "This is a good place for it," I thought to
myself. I walked my bike and myself a few feet forward until I'd centered myself into the middle of a thick ray of light, right there on my
bike path, right there just for me, right there, just for this. I felt it, the
light, I felt it's warmth and I connected to it and let it take me away,
upward towards its source. I gave myself to it. I just took a couple of
deep breaths, closed my eyes and let the power of it connect with my
spirit and let it just take me, and just like always, it did. "Heavenly
Father God, thank you for my soul and its connection to you. Thank
you for all the wonder and magic, this day and all the possibilities of
finding love for all of us all throughout the day. Protect us all from
fear. Help us all in all that we do and be especially with those who are
in crisis and fear. Thank you for this wonderful place in space and
time." Then, after a few more seconds of stillness and quiet, enjoying
the sensation of pure connection, I pushed and glided all the way
back home carrying with me the freshly recharged connection to
myself and the everything beyond.

It was about eight-thirty a.m. when I finally sat down at my desk.
Fifteen minutes earlier when I got back home I'd made a quick glance
into my office and had noticed that the digital readout on my business
phone line had recorded one message. I decided that that was work
whatever it was and it would have to wait ten more minutes until I
had a chance to shower, make myself a bagel and down a glass of
orange juice. Then, settled at my desk and sharing the last of my
bagel with my dog I hit the play button for line 2.

It was the voice of one of my best friends, Dave Purlis. Both of us
had in one way or the other spent most of our working careers in the
data processing business. Dave worked in programming and manage-
ment while I was a marketing type. "Hey Jack... It's, Dave, I've got
some bad news...This is a bad way to let you know... there's not a
good way...but...I know you'd want to know, as soon as possible."
Dave's words were coming out of him like the sounds a car makes just

149

as its about to run out of gas, sputtering ,he labored to continue, "Johnny Harrison killed himself Sunday night…This is so terrible! Apparently… he was on the phone with Brenda when he did it…That's all we know right now…Give me a call later…when you get a chance."

Feelings and thoughts all hit at the same time and as the stammered message finally ended I was bent forward in my chair seeing only the face of my dog looking up in anticipation of the last bit of our bagel. My breath mouthed the words, "oh my God…" Less than an hour earlier I was standing in the middle of the forest, to me, a place more beautiful than any Cathedral ever constructed by man. I don't know why but I remember thinking out loud, "matter can not be created or destroyed", I thought about Johnny and his hunting dogs, all those long, drawn out conversations we'd had over seven years while I'd worked for him. I had just heard that Johnnie was dead but I could not picture him that way. Some things take a while to get used to. Other things have nothing to do about "getting used to". I thought about how wonderfully nuts the guy was sometimes and of some of the things that made me think that. I could see him in his charcoal grey business suit, he always looked like a million dollars. He had everything, and I mean everything going for him. I could see him that last day he worked as my boss, late in the afternoon, leaning into my office cubical, saying that he was going to be gone for a couple of weeks, to take care of some personal business. I remember how stressed he looked, like he was just about to start shaking somehow, as he told me to tell everybody else. I wondered at the time, what else could happen to him? Just about three years ago, that was the last time I would ever see him.

And now this, I was as emotionless as if someone had handed me a memo that was intended for somebody else. Then the image started to sink in. The madness of it swallowed me whole.

I guess I was just mad that Johnny had lost it so bad as to go to that extreme. But I was not surprised; there was no surprise in me at all. I thought about that and I felt like I was going to cry, slings and arrows, outrageous fortune, Hamlet to Harrison. I understood immediately why he did what he did. Maybe I would of done the same thing? Maybe I would of done it a lot sooner? Yeah, I probably would have. The things some of us have to live with are just not livable with all of us who have to live with them, these things. I know that doesn't make any sense but that is what I'm talking about here, things that make no sense, but do. Things that make no sense but do. Let's see if I can relate all this in a way you might be able to understand. Most of us are raised to think, to believe that taking your own life is, that the act of doing it, is inexcusable and violates all religious laws. Probably you've heard that you won't be allowed to go to Heaven if you kill yourself, Purgatory maybe, if you believe that way. If you commit suicide you won't be able to live after you die. Philosophically you could spend the rest of your life in that discussion, be my guest, but it's a moot point somehow after the fact, right here, right now. All I can say is that I believe its much easier to get to heaven if you don't have to go through hell to get there. Not all of us are so fortunate.

Most of the time that I worked for Johnny things could not of been better. He brought out a lot of the good there was in me to the surface and we all prospered. Some of the things I think you need to be successful in any kind of business venture is a cohesion of people, personalities and the sharing of specific goals along with the intelligence and determination to achieve the various goals. We had all that in spades. We had it so good that we hardly talked about it. Some mornings I go into Johnny's office and we'd talk about everything but business. Additionally, Johnny and I traveled all over the United States together. Every year we made our objectives and got to go, along with our wives and sometimes our kids, to places we'd probably never go to otherwise. We went to Hawaii three times and other places just as exotic and fun. We got to know each other's families and we shared our concerns our fears, the everyday mundane and the sometimes-monumental problems we all share sometimes as human beings living in such a complex world. We supported each other in these ways and even though Johnnie was ten years younger than me I learned to respect his wisdom and judgment. I had grown up in the city and he a rural Alabama farm. Johnny was the first person I'd ever met who suggested to me that there was a world out there beyond my conception of bicycles. One Christmas, I had purchased as presents for my young children, two inexpensive bicycles from Wal-Mart. I was telling Johnny about it and in almost an insulting way stated quite mater-of-fact-ly to me "that the wheels on the bikes that they sold over at Wal-Mart weren't even round." I didn't believe him so he told me to first chance I got turn the bicycles up-side-down and spin the wheels as fast as I could. If they wobbled, that would mean that the wheels were not true, that meant that the spokes had to be adjusted until the wobbling stopped. Then the wheels would be in balance. Then they'd be round. It was a "who cares" for me at the time, but eventually I tried what he said. He was right, the kids' tires were no where near close to being true. It's just an example of things Johnny knew about that I didn't. I really didn't even believe him one day when he was doing his road biking before work and told me he had ridden twenty miles that morning. Twenty miles, on a bicycle? But it was true. This was long before I became interested myself in mountain biking.

We talked about many serious things too, divorce, marriage, death, our parents, religion. Johnny and I both were atheists back then. Things had happened to people who we loved that should not of happened. My mother died most horribly from cancer, Johnny's brother had died of AIDS. Johnny himself had gone through a divorce when he was much younger and seldom saw his daughter. All pretty tame stuff as to what was going to happen in the life of my good friend.

Mostly Johnny loved to talk about quail hunting. He used to joke that "if I didn't want to talk about bird dogs or shotguns I needed to go someplace else because those were the only things really important in life." We loved to talk about our dogs, his was named Sue and she was a beauty and she could hunt. Both of us were married and loved our wives very much. Johnny was devoted completely to Brenda and she to him. As I mentioned our business took us all over the country. I can't tell you how many women attempted more than a business relationship with Johnny. He really looked like he could of stepped off the cover of GQ. It was funny sometimes watching him maneuver himself out of in front and away from women who too obviously wanted a bit more than there data processed. They didn't know that to Johnny his marriage was an anchor and he respected and loved Brenda too much to let anybody jeopardize their relationship. He was adamant about it. It was real. While I was going through my separation and divorce Johnny did everything he could think of to encourage me to do what ever it took for me to stay married but in the end, when I had to give it up, he supported me there too. I owed Johnny for things I would never be able to repay him for.

I recall one day when he pops into my cube and asks me if I'm doing anything important. This is of course code for "let's get out of here." We get in his big pickup truck and we're headed up to Crane Hill, Alabama, where he is from. He says he needs to drop by his folks' house and just doesn't want to drive all that way by himself. It was about an hour's drive from our office. It was kind of neat. On the way up there he's telling me that his dad, who's retiring from farming and "the chicken business" had bought this big deluxe camper trailer thing and after all these years of farming he and his mother were going to see the world from this camper. His mom and dad's retirement would start with a "grand tour." Only problem is that Johnny is sure that his mother wants no part of it and is looking to get out of an almost fifty-year-old marriage. And, like a lot of us sometimes, his dad was in complete denial. Anyway, we get there.

Crane Hill, Alabama is really out in the country, it's beautiful up there and I'm just really enjoying the visual aspect of country living while Johnny talks to his father about what I don't know. His dad is built like one who's spent most of his life like you'd expect. In his sixties, he still looks strong and viable even with a bit of a gut. He greet-

ed me warmly with a firm handshake as he and Johnny began to con-
verse good naturally for a few minutes. About then Johnny's mother
comes outside looking like she's ready to go for a jog. She's dressed
for it too, the outfit, the shoes and a Sony Walkman. She's polite as
we are introduced but at the same time she's focusing on her exercise
as she puts on the headphones and heads down the blacktop road in
front of their house and is quickly out of site. She really looked good.

A few minutes later we're back in the pickup and headed back to
the office when Johnny says, "I don't know if my old man's going be
able to handle it. He doesn't have a clue." I knew what he meant,
what it looked like. The sight of two people going in different directions; I recognized and realized that the only time people usually recognize such things is in other people. It takes a while sometimes, it's
hardest to see when its happening to you, yourself, your own marriage. Johnny sure saw it easily enough. We both would hope that it
would work out. That is what people always hope. That's what hope
is, the believing that there is a chance that things will be all right, a
way will be found. Sometimes there is, sometimes there isn't.

How can you tell?

PHOTO BY BRUCE HYER

About the Author

Wayne Lankford is the author of The Bike Path. He lives right outside of Birmingham, Alabama. He graduated from The University of West Georgia. This is the first of what he hopes will become a series of books about connectivity and mountain biking.

Printed in the United States
1420900005B/283-327

9 780974 512501